Create

Transform What You Know
Into <u>How You Get Paid</u>

Jason Drohn

Jason Drohn

DEDICATION

To Chelsey and Sebastian.

For always being the place I call home.

Table of Contents

INTRODUCTION

Welcome to CREATE: Get Paid To Share What You Know.

First of all, I'd like to thank you for picking up this book. The lessons inside will help you create your very own 'offer' that you can sell online; like an eBook, video course, or audio course. We'll also spend some time on the coaching, consulting and event side as they are ways to monetize your skills and expertise even though they aren't necessarily product-based.

The first section of this book is largely based around on the planning and discovery phase of the process. That will help you discover what type of offer you're planning on creating, what audience you'll be serving, and how you'll go about fulfilling your product once you have buyers in the door.

Phase Two is the build phase… In other words, building your website, writing your sales copy, writing your email copy, and doing all the things necessary to promote.

Then, Phase Three is getting traffic... In other words, finding buyers for your offer! That's where the rubber meets the road and it's so much fun...

Now, I do have to warn you. There are parts of this book that might seem boring or overly complex. Don't let that stop you. This book outlines the process to building an information-based business, and what you need to do at every step. Make no mistake – it's a process. It's systematic.

This book is meant to be action-oriented, and you'll be able to make progress at your own pace as we go along... Make notes along the journey. Answer the questions that are posed in the chapters. Have fun along the way!

After all, the outline contained in this book will help you reach millions of people with your message. All you have to do is put something together for them that they'll love!

Now, I would be remiss if I didn't mention something...

This entire book is about making money with your skills, experience, knowledge and passion DIGITALLY. Why then, are you reading this book in its physical form?

The answer is simple. This material started as a digital course back in 2012. It was structured as a video course and then, after thousands of people had been through the material, I realized that the Internet had become so easy to use and eBooks so commonplace, that a Kindle and physical book version made sense.

So, after many rounds of edits and updates, it's ready!

With that being said, let's get into it. The first thing we'll do is go through a Discovery exercise. It's something we do with our clients quite often and should help you pull together your 'assets,' as we call them.

PART ONE: DISCOVERY

Your Skills and Talents

To sell digital products, namely informational offers like ebooks, video courses, memberships and the like, you need to be an expert at some level.

Does that mean you must be *the* expert? No. But you need to be reasonably skilled and have more expertise than the person who's buying your stuff!

…And things that you are good at are going to be what drives your product creation early on. Creating eBooks, courses, and information will be the easy part for you. If you're an expert in your field or whatever it is that you do, awesome! Without much help or guidance on your particular subject, you'll be able to get the information out and organized fairly quickly, and passion will drive you throughout the process.

If you are creating a product and hiring a ghostwriter to do the work, you are going to at least want to take an interest in the information that you'll be packaging up as a product. After all, you are paying someone to write all about it, and you'll have to work with the material for the next few years…

That this section is really about, is you.

This creation process is designed to work around your skills and talents, so we're going to start with some questions. Be truthful in your answers and make sure to write them down. I recommend that you have a notebook dedicated to it, that way you can keep your thoughts organized in one place. If you take the time to organize your project first, or at least the different parts of it, the creative process will unfold a lot more naturally.

Outlining a thought process, ideas, or creating a mind map can help you put your thoughts into words. I often find that the hardest part of the 'creation' process is the outline or the mindmap itself. Once the mindmap is done, all of the thinking has already been accomplished so all you have left to do is to fulfill.

If you brainstorm and use mind maps correctly, they minimize the product creation process from months or years to days or hours, and it'll be that much easier to go to market when the time comes!

Here's an example mind map that I actually used to create this book and the associated material:

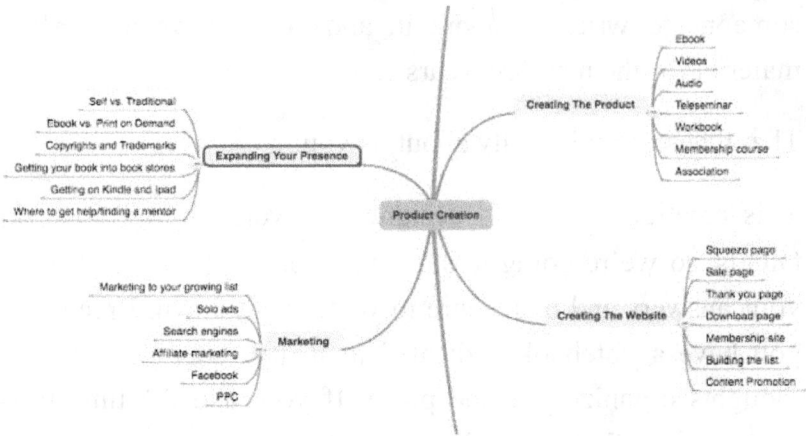

A mind map with central node "Product Creation" connecting to:

- **Creating The Product**: Ebook, Videos, Audio, Teleseminar, Workbook, Membership course, Association
- **Expanding Your Presence**: Self vs. Traditional, Ebook vs. Print on Demand, Copyrights and Trademarks, Getting your book into book stores, Getting on Kindle and Ipad, Where to get help/finding a mentor
- **Marketing**: Marketing to your growing list, Solo ads, Search engines, Affiliate marketing, Facebook, PPC
- **Creating The Website**: Squeeze page, Sale page, Thank you page, Download page, Membership site, Building the list, Content Promotion

Most people don't give themselves enough credit where it's due.

The information you have in any field or area of expertise isn't just of value to you, it's of value to anyone who seeks the information out.

You have skills, experiences, and talents that others desire, and those people can shorten their own learning or growth curves by learning what you already know... That's what people will pay for – the transformation! Your product can give them exactly what they need and want.

One of my favorite authors, Brendon Burchard says that, "Even if you're two steps ahead of the person behind you, you still have information and knowledge that could be beneficial to them." You don't necessarily need to be a guru or an expert to help them. In fact, it's better not to be because then there aren't any preconceived notions about who you are or what you provide.

If you have a couple little tools, tricks or strategies that help someone move forward, then you're providing a service to them. This puts you in a place where you can make quite a bit of money selling what you know as long as it's packaged up the right way and available for sale!

The followers you gather (read: your customers) will be grateful, loyal, and come back for more which means there's always room for additional offers to make to them!

Here are some questions that I want you to answer:

1. **What do you do for a living?** Are you in a professional services field? Maybe you're in construction. I used to be a semi-truck driver. I don't have any products in the semi-truck driving space, although I have worked with a couple people that do.

2. **What experience do you have from a professional standpoint?** Is it something that you went to school for? Did you go to a trade school or anything like that to further your knowledge in the subject?

3. **What brings you pleasure?** What do you have fun doing? What subjects do you like? All hobbies have followings online. It's not out of the question to develop a product for model train collectors, because they are out there. Then you just have to tap into that space online and start selling your product.

4. **What is it that you really enjoy doing, that other people also enjoy doing?** More specifically, how can you help them get to where you are or get to a better place?

5. **What would you do if you were working for free?** This is a question that I like to ask myself, because, frankly, I would be doing what I'm doing right now. I just love what I do. So

what is it that you love doing? If you had to go to work and not receive a paycheck, what would you enjoy doing for years and years?

6. **What are some of the experiences you've lived through?** Have you had a very intense trial or tribulation in your life? Have you had a particularly low point that you can help other people through? How did that look? Are there people that are experiencing the same particular low point, the same pain in their life that you can help them through?

7. **Was there a point where you were struggling and you made it out?** It might be a financial problem, something emotional or trouble with a relationship? Some of the best digital products in the world come from a place of pain. So, if you've lived through something, you can put together action steps on beating it, and teach others!

If that's not enough, here's another line of questioning; what do people routinely ask you about?

Maybe you're really good with computers, so folks ask you about cleaning up their PC's and making them run faster, how to fix a hard drive or write new partitions. Maybe you are really good with home theatre installation since you researched and installed your own in your basement. Perhaps you've struggled with getting dates because of your erratic work schedule. How then, did you end up meeting your spouse? Your knowledge and experiences are valuable. Sure, maybe your exact method won't work for everybody, but your trials and tribulations are worth sharing if the end result was successful.

More thoughts and questions that may lead you to ponder over your passions:

- What are some of the successes that I've had?

- What have I done in the past that has really influenced where I am at now?

- What are my goals and my aspirations?

- Where do I want to be in one year, five years or ten years?

- Do I relate to one group of people more than another?

- Do I consider myself following one person? Look at who your role models and the people you are following online. What do they have in common? What do you and the other followers have in common? Sometimes that's a really good way of pinpointing where you're going.

I've always found that envisioning what my life would look like in the future is a great way of figuring out what I want to do now. It's also a really good way of figuring out who the audience is for your product!

- **If you had all the money in the world, what would you do?** What would you buy? Where would you live? What would your family look like? What kind of cars would you drive? What time would you wake up in the morning? What brings you joy?

And then, following up on that question, ask yourself:

- How can I generate the cash flow to live my dream life?

Many people start with something they may not be great at, but are passionate about.

Passion drives you to perfection, and the result can be success.

Let's say you enjoy taking pictures. If photography is something you are passionate about, it will be that passion that puts you ahead of the game in learning more and more about it. You then could teach others how to take the perfect pictures. You can travel, take pictures, and sell them to National Geographic or to stock photography sites like iStockPhoto.com.

Each subject has a doorway which can lead you into transmuting your passion into money, and that is what the rest of this book is designed to show you.

I actually just received an email newsletter from Digital Photography School, founded by Darren Rowse. I have been online long enough to remember when DPS wasn't even created. And to know that Darren Rowse is where he is today because of his passion for photography.

Darren Rowse started ProBlogger.net, which is where I first started following him. Then he started his Digital Photography School because of his passion for digital photography. Darren went from being a start-up blogger to now having of hundreds of thousands of email newsletter subscribers, simply because of his driving passion for photography. Now, he has an entire team of editors and makes money on his site through affiliate products, advertising, and selling his own products. There are ways for everyone to become successful when passion for a subject leads them to pursue ways of getting their knowledge to their audience.

Since you are reading this book, my guess is you already have the answers to a lot of my questions. You probably have an idea for a book, an eBook, PDF, or something similar that you can put together pretty quickly. Maybe, you've already started writing or creating something and it's sitting on your hard drive, ready for the next step.

Or, perhaps you have an idea for educating others though a video training course, membership site, or audio program. Even if you have tried to put something together already and just want a guide to help you sell and package it, you are in the right place!

All you really need is a direct, strategic method of creating, packaging and selling your digital product, so that you can start to cash in…

Digital products are:

- Easy to create

- Require very little capital expenditure to get started

- Simple to fulfill

- Highly valued as there are no delivery times

- Cutting edge, since updates can be published instantly

Physical products can also be successful, but there are lots of roadblocks when it comes to getting one started…

The design phase of a physical product can be laborious. There is upfront expense, even if that's printing, publishing and shipping. You might need warehousing or sales teams. And really, with video being so easy and cheap, information products have no business being sold physically!

After all, you can do high quality videos right from your iPhone or Android device!

… Unless it's a book, of course. Physical, bound books will always be a mainstay in the marketplace just because people still love to feel and touch them.

Personally, I prefer physical books but even they start as a digital file, uploaded to CreateSpace.com or the like. There is hardly no cost there!

To start, we need to define your position as an expert in your field. It'll help you organize the way you deliver your content to your audience, find and engage your prospects, and how you'll connect with them in a personal way even if it is automated!

Now, let's dig in a little deeper.

- Who do you want to work with? Do you have an ideal client – the type of person that you'd enjoy working with?

- What do you want to teach your audience? What do you want to teach the members of your site or your followers?

- What kind of information can you share that you already have access to or that you've already created? Take inventory of what you have, because you might find that it's a lot easier to create your product if you're just stitching the pieces together!

- How are you going to make a difference in your customers' lives? That's a big question. How are you going to positively impact your followers so that you help them make a transformation? And how is their life going to be better because of you?

- What are you going to be able to do for them? That's the bottom line, after all. What will you be able to do for your customers? If you can't answer that question, nobody's going to buy from you. You need to improve their life in some way…

- What is the best way to present your material? If it's a three step tutorial on how to take better photographs, can you present it on a webinar? Is it something that they're going to be able to look at and understand or are you going to need to do a YouTube video that walks them through the whole process?

As we get into creating products and getting leads for your business, we'll get into more detail… But there are a few things you need to keep in mind throughout the process so that you can make the biggest impact in the lives of your customers.

In order to attract an audience and ultimately sell something, you need to have an idea of what your audience is going through and why they need to know what you do. In order to create a successful product, you need to truly understand what your potential buyer wants out of the information so that you can sell it effectively.

The connection and understanding between you and your buyer is going to reflect in your website copy, your sales copy, and your email copy, and it is the only way you are going to be able to sell anything.

Your audience needs to be the reason you do what you do. Don't treat your followers like a list of emails. Asking your followers "What can I do to help?" is the one thing that will get you repeat customers, reliable followers, and interest worldwide.

… Not to mention they'll be the source of some of the best ideas you have in terms of new products and new offers!

Setting Goals

When you're building something your passionate about, sometimes it is easy to get lost in the process and end up somewhere you never intended. A campaign might not go the way you wanted it to or a partnership goes the wrong direction.

So far, you probably have a pretty solid idea about what you can provide as far as a product that'll benefit your audience. If you have an idea of how you are going to help them, you are off to a good start, but take a second to remember yourself in this equation.

Go ahead and answer these questions. Give yourself reasons that will solidify in your mind where you want to be BECAUSE of the business that you're starting...

- Where do you see yourself in 6 months or 12 months? Three years. Five years?

- What will you enjoy about doing what you're doing for a living?

- How are you making money – selling products, selling services? Will you be getting digital payments or checks in the mail?

- What kind of house are you living in? Big? Small? A condo? A farm?

- What does your family look like? Your spouse? Your kids?

- Where are your kids going to school? Private? Public?

- What kind of clothes are you wearing? Designer? Something fancy?

- What does your street look like? Who are your neighbors?

- Do you live on the water or in the middle of the woods?

- What kind of car are you driving?

- Where did you just go on vacation?

- What does your workday look like? Do you go to an office? Do you work out of your house?

- Do you have a place to record video and audio? Do you do live workshops or events?

- How do you engage your audience on a daily, weekly or monthly basis?

- How big is your email list? Your buyer's list? Your prospects?

- Do you speak at conferences or travel the speaking tour? Do you attend meet-ups or networking events?

- What is your ideal day? How is it structured?

- What time do you wake up in the morning? What do you have for breakfast?

If you have any other thoughts that come to mind, write them all down, and plan out what your life is going to look like in a couple years.

These might sound like trivial or stupid questions, but having a set of goals for yourself really puts things in perspective, so you continuously have something to work towards.

Goals will change as you become more and more successful, and that's okay. Looking back, I can now see that I have moved in a drastically different direction than where I originally thought I was going to go. However, my goals are still being met.

Personally, one of my original goals was that I wanted to get a Hummer H2. That was one of my 'Destinations.'

When the time came to get a new car, we didn't go H2 route but made the decision to buy a Jeep instead. At the time, it was just a better choice.

Even though we didn't get a Hummer, my goal was satisfied because we did buy a Jeep! The goal was met, and the need was filled, so I crossed it off my list! (I did, however, buy a Hummer H2 since!)

What I'm trying to say is your goals will change. Your needs, wants, and interests change. Likes and dislikes will change. Don't let it bother you if you don't reach a goal you set for yourself five years ago. Let it work for you throughout those five years, and adapt if you need to.

There's really something very powerful about writing your goals down. By knowing and writing down what you want, your mind actually starts to take action in your goals, and figuring out how it's going to attain them. This isn't some 'woo woo' law of attraction thing either. Once you're aware that you want something, you will make the decisions necessary for achieving it.

Not to mention, it's much more satisfying when you can cross your goals off your list one by one.

By realizing where you want to be in life, you'll start to put the processes in place that allow you to get there. There is one key though… The only way you'll ever hit your goals is by actually doing something.

It's not rocket science, but you do need to do something in order to start checking goals off of your list!

That's one of the reasons this book is so much about taking action and moving in the direction of creating and launching your product!

Focused Action

The difference between people with massive success and people without it, is focus.

When I first started my business, I tried so many different things. I threw stuff at the wall and hoped it would stick. It wasn't until I focused on one path until I actually started succeeding in business.

I've spoken to many different people over the years – both prospective clients and members - who are wishy-washy about what they want to do with their life. They want to be successful and wealthy, but it seems that they change course in favor of something new every few months...

They want to be thin, but they jump from their workout plan to a new diet and back again.

Focus is key.

Consistency in how you approach your tasks and forgoing the "new" distraction will ensure success in the long run.

7 or so years ago, I was trying desperately to make something work online. It was 2009 and the bottom fell out of my business and so many other businesses around the world.

I ended up building a whopping 35 websites, all geared towards DIFFERENT ways to generating revenue online.

What ended up happening was I had so many websites and not nearly enough money, time, and energy to keep them all up. I ended up not doing any of them the right way and absolutely remained broke.

Then, I learned to focus my efforts. I started focusing my time on affiliate marketing. Affiliate marketing in and of itself, was all I did. I would stay up until the early morning hours and do nothing except writing content for search engines and affiliate marketing.

That effort led me into information products.

I then launched a few eBooks on my own that did really well, because I understood how to rank sites in Google, thanks to the affiliate marketing.

Shortly after, other people started to see what I was doing, and many wondered how I had achieved such massive results.

So, rather than talk to every single person who was interested in my methods, I focused on creating a course, investing the time initially into creating a course, and marketing it to my audience.

That way, folks had the opportunity to learn in a structured way and then follow up with any questions that they had!

Now, in order to sell anything online, you need to understand your target market and intended audience. You have to empathize with them, understand what they need and appeal to their interests…

In other words, you need to know how to relate to them.

If you are creating a digital product without your target audience specifically in mind, they may never even see your product, let alone think it's for them.

Through the entire process, your intent has to be to reach your target market. You have to write specifically for them, advertise for them, and write your sales copy for them.

There are many people out there thinking, "I want to sell this to everybody. Everybody needs this product." You might have even heard similar statements on shows like, "Shark Tank."

If you are think the whole world needs your stuff and you create sales material for the whole world, you're not going to sell anything.

Any investor or marketer who knows what they're doing will tell you the exact same thing. There are many brilliant people out there who are broke, simply because they failed to focus their efforts on their target market.

One of my good friends, Mike Hill, actually just sent out a video the other day. He said:

> "There are millionaires and there are hundred-aires. The difference between the millionaires and the hundred-aires is not information. The difference is that the millionaires do one thing and do it over and over and over again. And sometimes they're too stupid to realize that there are other things that

they could be doing, but they're millionaires. The hundred-aires try to get all the information and arrange it and they spend their entire life in pursuit of knowledge and information. They don't actually make a dime."

What happens is that the brilliant people who are broke have failed to focus. They have a great idea, but failed to do anything that make their target market feel as though they offered a solution to their problem...

Unfocused people see that something has worked for someone, and go off chasing the next, newest thing.

The reality is though, there is only so much time in a day.

With 60 minutes to an hour, 24 hours in a day, seven days a week, and 52 weeks a year, how much of that time are you wasting? How much of that time is being used to focus your efforts and bring in cash the front door in your business?

It's too easy to waste time examining spreadsheets, graphs, charts, social media, and all that other busy work that feels necessary but doesn't actually make you any money.

How much time are you spending avoiding any work activities will actually move your business forward? ...That will actually help you accomplish your goals faster? ...Time spent doing anything other than the work you should be doing?

The most important question to ask yourself is "What am I doing that's making money?" After all, in business that's the bottom line.

For me and my business, I call this the "Quickest Path To Cash Strategy," or QPC for short. Whenever we start a new business or a new project, I always ask myself what do we have ready right now that can produce revenue? Then, I move forward on that.

Performing work tasks on a day to day basis that makes you money and improves your life is what you need to focus on. Things you need to ponder daily are:

- Where am I finding success?

- What am I doing right now that's generating income?

- What feels right – as in it's easy or it makes the best use of my skills.

You need to either be working on profitable ventures or relaxing. There really is no in between. Doing the dishes, mowing your lawn, it's all busy work that you perhaps shouldn't be doing! That is, unless you enjoy doing it of course.

I find the working with my hands – building stuff, mowing the lawn, doing the dishes – helps me process. I have some of my best ideas in the garage or out in the yard. So for me, that stuff is vital to my process. For you, it might not be!

My guess is that you are filling your time with pseudo-actions or other activities that look like action and getting things done, but they don't move you any closer to the goals you've set for yourself.

Then, after you've worked all day long, you spend the time you should be relaxing thinking about work and money... And the time you spend working, you feel guilty about all the things you're missing out on with your family!

There are ways to train yourself to improve focus. Try this very simple exercise four times a day:

1. Set your calendar to send you a reminder at different intervals asking you the very simple question, "Am what I doing right now making me money?"

2. If the answer is no too many times in a row, you need to improve your focus. If your answer is yes, they you're on the right track. If your answer is a reoccurring yes, you're probably finding that your workdays are shortening now, and you're spending more and more time doing what you enjoy.

Getting there takes time though. You end up having an incredible life because what you're focusing on during work time is work related, and what you're doing during relaxation time is actually fun!

Your Action Plan

Having a good action plan is the nuts and bolts approach of taking action... It's knowing what you need to do and why you need to do it.

Having goals and aspirations are what you ultimately strive for, but you need to DO something to get there.

Having an action plan lets you see where you are going ahead of time. It's a predetermined set of actions that get you where you want to go.

Without a good action plan, your success is going to be much harder to attain. If you are starting without an action plan, you aren't necessarily going to know how to to where you want to go, because it hasn't been broken down into easy, quantifiable steps.

Everyone has goals, but you aren't going to reach them without knowing how you'll start moving toward them. You may want to walk on the moon someday, but I can guarantee that'll never become a reality unless you have a pretty good idea of what you need to do next!

The same principles apply online. Digital products, affiliate marketing, and building an email list all require a thorough action plan. Selling copies of your course and marketing your product online – it all requires an action plan.

Course developers and product creators have been teaching it for years, and this is the third part of the little trifecta that I call strategic success.

You can look at some of the most successful people in the world and this is exactly what they do. They have solid, stable action plans. They always know what they need to do, when they need to do it, and how to achieve success from it. Strategic success is really just that; goals, focus, and action.

Here's how it happens.

You plot your goals and write down exactly what you want and where you want to go in the next week, month, year or five years, whichever timeframe you think you need to begin with.

Then, examine your focus. Tell yourself out loud "These are the goals I want to hit and this is what I want to focus on to achieve those goals."

From there, plan your actions based on your goals and focus. Here's a page out of my last book, Phoenix Formula:

My goal: Live in a 10,000 square foot house in Tennessee and work with the people I want to.

My primary action: Put together a training course with traffic, conversion strategies and lead generation at the heart of it all.

My action plan: (my action plan would look like this)

1. Register a domain name.

2. Get a website built.

3. Create a freebie report or something to give away to generate leads.

4. Create video content for the course.

5. Get it edited and encoded.

6. Put together a marketing plan and affiliate program.

7. Make money.

This action plan might look foreign to you right now, but it won't be by the time you reach the end of this book.

It might almost seem too simple, but it's actually the same blueprint that you'll be using to create digital products and it's responsible for selling millions of dollars worth or products and services over the decade that I've been in business.

From the action plan, I would it break down into 'to-do' lists.

So, the second action item in my action plan is to "Get a website built." Pretty daunting stuff, right? If you don't have much experience online, it might seem like a pretty complicated process.

Before even getting started, some people might get turned off. If you're thinking "Where do I start?" you have two options. You can either hire out, or do it yourself.

The first thing you are going to need to do is figure out what you want your website to look and feel like.

- What features do you want?

- What do you want the site to look like?

- Do you have a logo and a tagline? (Do you need one?)

- What do you want to sell on your site?

- How are you going to handle payments? PayPal, Merchant Processor, or a site like ClickBank.

If you're going to hire it out, you can:

- Find a local company to do it for you (there are seemingly hundreds of them in every city!)

- Hire a relative who has a blog or a bit of programming background and have them do it for you.

- Post the job on freelancing and outsourcing sites like Upwork.com.

If you are going to do it on your own, you can set up a pretty seamless website for a few bucks by purchasing website hosting and installing WordPress, which is a free blog and content management system.

Then, after your website is up and running, cross it off your action plan!

As you move through your action plan, you're working your way down the plan and getting closer to your goal overall!

With an action plan, the thinking process is taken out of the equation. You can just sit down during work time, review what you need to do that day, and either get it done or figure it out!

Now, I am going to deconstruct the process of building a digital product for you in this book, so you don't have to worry about the process. What I want you to focus on is your own little blueprint of how you are going to take action, and start achieving your goals.

Here are some questions I want you to answer to help get you started on your action plan:

- How does your digital product play into your business? Is it the core offer or do you have upsells in place?

- Who are you going to target in your marketing so that they take notice and buy it?

- How are you going to do what's required for a successful digital product launch? I'm going to be giving you action plans and blueprints for creating digital products, but consider how it's going to work in your whole business and what you need to do to put it all together.

- Are you going to sell from the stage?

- Are you going to use it as an up sell for your book?

- Are you going to use it as a lead generation piece for a website or for your company?

It's really up to you, which is the fun part! Just make sure your product or offer works into the rest of your marketing mix. After all, once it's done it's an asset for you and your business!

Your Target Market

One of your most important considerations at this point, is your target market. **In other words, WHO are you going to be selling to...**

Researching a market is usually the 'make or break' point when you're growing a business online. It's also one of the biggest reasons you hear so many people talking about 'niche research.'

Niche research is all about finding the subgroups within a market, or those small segments within a large overall market. For example, there is a niche of powerlifting enthusiasts, and it's a small market. But, it's part of a much larger health and fitness market.

The reason why niche research is so important is because there are millions upon millions of people who could buy your product or service. But will they? That's the question. By targeting the right type of buyer, you're able to put your offer in front of the people who are most likely to buy.

As you get started, there will be markets and ideas that you'll have that aren't great to start off with because the market is too small to turn a profit. There simply isn't enough buyers there or they're too illusive to get in front of.

The absolute first thing you need to know though, is your market is probably not who you think they are...

Sure, they're overweight, stressed, broke, or trying to live a better lifestyle in some way, but do you really know them? Can you emphasize with them? Do you know what their world actually looks like?

This is where our goal planning exercise that we opened up with comes in handy. Here are some questions to ponder:

- Are they male or female?

- How old are they?

- Do they have long hair, short hair, stylish hair, disheveled hair?

- Do they wear nice clothes? Do they dress sloppy?

- What kind of shoes do they have on?

- What time did they leave for work in the morning?

- Did they have breakfast?

- What time did they wake up?

- Did they work out first thing in the morning? Do they work out?

- Did they check their email first thing?

- What kind of day do they have planned? Board meetings, taking the kids to a soccer game?

- What did they have for lunch?

- Do they eat junk food?

- Do they watching sitcoms?

- Do they talk to their friends on the phone?

- Do they do their own cleaning? Laundry?

- What is their afternoon like? Are they doing family stuff? Are they working? Are they not going to be home until 9:00 at night?

- Are they making dinner for their family or is it just TV dinners in front of the television?

- What do they do in the evening? Help their kids with homework? Spend time talking to their spouse?

These are all very telling things that you need to know about your target market before you move forward. It'll help you cater to them through your marketing, sales copy and your product!

- Where do they live? The suburbs, apartment, in the city? Trees? Pond? Big deck? Vaulted ceilings?

- What kind of car do the drive, a broken down SUV, a couple of mid-sized sedans, an Escalade, a Lamborghini?

My point is, you want to see your customer's life, and then view a snapshot of what life might be like for them every day. Then, you craft every single marketing message so that it affects them, from now on.

If it helps, give your avatar a name. Market to Bob, Jeff, or Jesse. It doesn't matter, just make him or her real. Make the messaging stand out to them because of who they are. Every blog post, every video, every email marketing message; they should ALL should focus specifically on your target market.

When you are able to tailor your marketing to your target market, your prospect will read your message and feel that you are talking directly to them. It's incredibly powerful. Try not to worry about what happens if someone fits directly into every word you say… The remarkable thing about the human brain is that it'll start to make up stories and substitute them for your words when you're on point with everything else! So, you'll sell them too!

In your prospects mind, they'll start to fill in the blanks between the information crafted for them, their lives and their problems. They'll start to fabricate experiences with your message in hand.

For instance, if I want to sell a personal development, 'Think and Grow Rich' type of product, I would probably have something along these lines in my sales copy:

> "You know what that feels like, to not have enough money in the bank to afford dog food, let alone your credit card payment. What I want to do is tell you how I broke free from all that disgrace and embarrassment and literally took back control of my life, making myself and my family whole again. I did it by…"

Chances are good that you'll catch the attention of your target audience if your marketing material comes close to the words you just read. You may have even had a period in your life where you scraped by to make a house payment or buy food. In your mind, you may have related the dog or with the children and fabricated a story around not being able to afford groceries or prescriptions or school supplies.

This feeling is what keeps you reading, making you feel uniquely tied to the person telling the story. Nail this one and it doesn't matter what you are selling, you'll be able to sell a lot of it.

All it takes is:

- **Step 1:** Visualizing your perfect customer.

- **Step 2:** Naming him or her.

- **Step 3:** Writing your sales message and ad copy directly for that person.

Your Competitors

Before we cover too much more ground, it's worth mentioning the competitive piece to business online... And why it really doesn't matter.

Ever since you decided to start your business, decided to go to business school, or talked to anyone about a business idea; you've probably been told that competition is an important part of figuring out whether you'll be successful or not.

If a space or niche is too competitive, you've been told to stay away. It's common to think that having too much competition in a market is bad because eventually the market corrects itself, and you'll be out of business.

Online, it is actually the opposite.

Finding a HUGE niche or category is key, because those mega-industries have the capability of supporting your business, as well as the thousands of other people in that space. Competition isn't always bad.

Some of the best markets in the world to get into are those wrought by competition. In fact, some of my closest friends and I only get into markets where there is a lot of competition because it means that there is quite a bit of money there.

There are a lot of people who think that if their idea was already built, there is no possibility that they can profit from it.

Nothing could be further from the truth.

Business spend incredible sums of money testing and growing a new product. They have to pay to educate their customers, expose people to a new brand, test marketing collateral, plus lots of other costs associated with launching something new…

It's not about a product being cool, innovative, or fun. It's more about making a difference in a customer's life, and making them believe the want and need it. New products and ideas pave the way for future competitors who will be launching in the same space.

Think about the iPad. Before the iPad, there were tablets on the market. They usually had a swiveling display and keyboard that would transform the 'laptop' into a tablet, and of course the display was a touch display like what we are now familiar with.

Sales for these tablets were lackluster.

… But then, the iPad was released. There was no keyboard, it had a touch display, and it could be used as a standalone unit. Within a year, the tablet industry took off tremendously, and the iPad served as the jumping off point.

Now every major tablet producing company competes against Apple and its iPad, some better than others. So even though Apple's iPad wasn't the first tablet on the market, it revolutionized the industry.

Smart people, smart entrepreneurs, and successful companies use the ground work that has already been laid out by their competitors to launch their own products and services. What competition tells you, is that the niche you're looking to get into is filled with cash paying customers.

Without competition, it might be best to rethink your product entirely!

You're a very smart person, but if no competition exists, there is a reason for it! Someone has probably already thought of what you are trying to do and failed. That, my friend, is why there's no competition.

Whenever I type a search term into Google and I don't see any competition, it makes me think twice. Maybe there isn't any money there or the idea has already been launched and failed. It is far better to get into a market that has competition and buyers than it is to think too far outside the box and sacrifice time and resources on something that's unproven.

If the market is not new and it's still uncompetitive there is probably one of the following problems:

- People aren't willing to spend money on a solution.
- The problem is being solved for free through some other means, like online searches.

- The majority of people don't know that a problem exists, and aren't willing to spend money to solve it.

- It's too expensive to find buyers and leads, and it doesn't work as a business model

There are hundreds of reasons why a product may not work in a market, but the clearest indicator you'll find is whether or not there are already competitors there.

If you find out there's little to no competition, go back to brainstorming. If you do find that there's competition in your field, start figuring out how you are going to enter the space. Look for ways to get in by solving problems that no one else is focusing on.

... If I can solve areas of weakness in other products and still provide the same value that other products provide, it's going to make my product really easy to sell.

Another way to enter a big market is by finding a great product in the market and piggybacking on its success. For example, say there is a $2,000 course that teaches customers how to get local consulting clients.

The majority of customers are not going to be able to afford a $2,000 course, so they don't buy it, despite wanting and needing the information.

So, by selling a competing product with similar or better information, you're already much further ahead because you know that the market exists and what they're willing to pay!

Some of the most competitive markets and the best to move into are:

- Relationship markets

- Health, fitness and weight loss

- Business, sales and marketing

- Finance and stock trading

- Personal development and self-help

- Survival and preparedness

- Pets

- Lifestyle

These markets are multi-billion dollar markets and it doesn't take much to create a million dollar offer if you follow the information in the rest of this book.

If you're looking to get into something that is more niche based, do some research to identify whether or not there is money in that market before you start investing time and money into it.

Here are some of the places I look for competition:

- Amazon.com – Search through books and Kindle Books to see how many other people have covered your topic. If necessary, buy the book(s) and go through them.

- Dummies.com – The Dummies books do A LOT of things right, including niche research. They have an entire research division who's only job is to figure out if a book or a niche has enough buyers. In other words, if there's a Dummies book covering roughly the same topic as you'd like to cover, you're in good company!

- Google.com – Do a search for your topic on Google, looking for ads in the right hand column. If you see some, you know that it's a profitable niche because people are spending money to advertise for that search term.

- Keyword research – There are a few keyword tools I like to use, including Google's Keyword Planner and WordTracker.com.

  Google's Keyword Planner helps you find groups of keywords and their search volume per month, so that you make an informed decision about whether or not your chosen niche is a good target.

  WordTracker gives you long tail keyword research that you can to figure out exactly what your prospects and customers search for.

  In each instance, you'll get a better idea of just how big your market is, on a country or global scale.

- ClickBank – Clickbank is the world's leading digital product retailer, offering publishers the ability to sell their digital products and providing affiliates and merchant access. Clickbank has products in many different niches and industries and will be a good tool for you to use to qualify your idea, and find the competition!

Market Research

Product research is incredibly important when it comes to building a successful online business. The research element is one of the most valuable pieces of the puzzle, and unfortunately it is always overlooked.

What we're looking for in this phase of the project is where we can sell our product, our offer, for once it's complete.

Find where ads seem to pop up on a regular basis, like:

- Google

- Facebook

- Pinterest

- Twitter

- Blog posts

- Websites you frequent

- Youtube

- Email lists you're subscribed to

- What we're looking for here is how to launch... Social media platforms can definitely help launch your product initially, in terms of paid traffic.

And after your offer is launched people will start doing product reviews, share their opinions on social media and help you get noticed.

When you begin putting your product into production, you really need to put some thought into what you can do to help people spread the word for you... Can you include share links? Can you give away some special bonus for folks who share your website with 3 friends? Can you put some functionality in place to 'waitlist' new free members?

Your Digital Presence

Presence in the market is really about what you have, your assets, in place. That includes having a website, an email list, a regularly updated blog, social profiles, etc. In short, your presence is what raises the awareness of your brand the and the problem that you'll be solving.

If you do not already have a presence in the market you want to get into, or if you're starting fresh; you'll need to build your presence online in order to attract customers and joint venture partners.

You'll also need to start building an email list so that you can go to market faster. Having a presence in the market isn't necessarily crucial, but you definitely need to have certain things set up correctly to launch successfully.

One thing that you'll need to think about before you launch a product is to establish yourself online... Wherever your prospects are, that's where you want to be. This includes a Facebook Page, Twitter, LinkedIn and getting ranked for at least your name, your company name and your product name in Google.

Having a searchable presence is always a reassuring thing to a customer who may be thinking about purchasing your product. They are going to want to see reputation, knowledge, experience, and anything else you have to offer.

In a lot of verticals, like coaching, consulting, freelancing and digital publishing, you really need to focus on creating yourself as a brand. Your content, courses, and products are an extension of the name you create for yourself.

Having a positive web presence and having people buzz about you ensures when they get wind of your new product, they are able to Google you and find that you come up as the expert, bottom line. People will search for your name, your company, your product, and product reviews.

Your customers, especially newer ones, will always look for proof and credibility of a product and your name, especially when buying online. The more credibility you gain, the more products you sell.

Credibility might be hard to define online nowadays, but having 'social proof' to provide to potential customers speaks volumes. Having 20,000 'likes' on your Facebook page might make a wary buyer feel more secure about purchasing, since 20,000 other people already like what you are doing.

Some people, no matter what 'social proof' you have, are just plain cautious when doing business online unless there is a significant bonding process that they go through before being asked to make a purchase.

Your web presence can be comprised of a number of things, but these are five things that I really suggest you having in place before you launch your product or service:

- **A blog or a website of your own, on your own domain name.** It can be your company name, your own name, or the name of your product. Search engines and prospective buyers like to see interactivity so the more you post relevant information that adds value to their life, the better you'll be in your prospects' eyes.

- **A Facebook page for your company or product.** You'll want to make sure to set up a Facebook Page showcasing your product, the things it can do, and the success stories you gather. This is an integral part of Facebook advertising as well!

- **Create a LinkedIn profile and business page.** LinkedIn is more of a business social network, but there are a growing number of people who will search for you in LinkedIn as a company or product owner. Make sure to set up a LinkedIn profile so that that base is covered.

- **Create a Twitter profile.** Twitter goes from being the red-headed stepchild to the media darling month by month. It's important for you to set up a Twitter profile and use it as often as you can muster. I for one don't get into Twitter much, but there are a growing number of people who love it for the transparency that it gives followers.

- **Create a YouTube channel and upload YouTube videos.** There's an incredible bonding that happens through video. Whether they're full motion videos or a voiceover with you talking to your computer (recording either with Camtasia or Screenflow), are incredibly powerful. Prospects get to hear your voice and see you, they get to read their body language and listen to verbal cues, all drawing them in closer to you.

It can be you sitting at your desk or you in front of a white board. It really doesn't matter. Good video really has a strong bonding element to it.

The sales process is the next step we will go through, and we will go into detail about how all of these 'web presence' elements come into play as they relate to converting traffic into buyers.

In any good sales process, audio and video is a big part. Webinars and sales videos are great tools that you need to have in your business. In "Convert," the next book in this series, we go into far more depth about the sales process and building sales funnels that convert.

Briefly though, webinars are a fantastic bonding tool for you and your viewers. For the prospective buyer, they get to watch you work your magic for the duration of the webinar. You get the chance go through the material and training, plus it gives you the opportunity to answer questions.

It's the perfect time to go through your pitch to sell your product or course.

To put it plainly, a webinar is one of the simplest sales tools that you have at your disposal.

In addition to webinars, you can also utilize tele-seminars. They work okay… Not as great as a webinar since it lacks that on-screen video component with the viewer.

A tele-seminar requires your attendees to dial into a phone number so you can talk to all of the attendees at once.

The other thing that is essential for building your digital presence is having you email autoresponder set up correctly. Email autoresponders are targeted and scheduled email messages that you set up in advance of someone receiving them.

When your prospects sign up for your list, they receive an automatic message from you that you have set up ahead of time. You have the ability to them email them using daily automatic messages, if you want to. It's all predetermined by you, so you control when, why and how they get the information ahead of time. It's simple and easy to do, and it's the glue that holds your sales funnel together.

Blog content that people can read and relate to themselves is also powerful. It can be tied with video, audio, PDF's or other tools that people can download and consume. Using free reports, PDF's and book chapters is helpful for your prospects, because you can actually have them read or watch that material for 50-90 minutes rather than watching a video for a only five minutes. Plus, you can include links and use language that attracts a prospects attention to compel them to buy more quickly.

Touch points are another aspect that you're going to want to utilize. Touch points are the specific places that get you in front of your prospect.

Touch points can include:

- Seeing you on Facebook

- Seeing your banner on one of their favorite websites (through retargeting, of course!)

- Getting an email from you

- Seeing a YouTube video of you

- Checking out your blog

- Being sent to your LinkedIn Profile

- And any number of other scenarios

Realistically, the more they see you in places they frequent, the more likely they are to trust you and your message.

This can lead to them purchasing from you more quickly and spending more over the long term.

For those of you who feel you are a little more experienced, you know that this can be pulled off through 'retargeting' or 'remarketing,' but we will save that conversation for later.

The other aspect of touch points to consider is the medium through which your message is being conveyed, either video, audio, or text. People grasp concepts differently, and a both video and audio can be used to sell to people differently than text would. The same goes for the person who would rather read than listen… The more text they can get their hands on, the better.

You have to create for as many different types of prospects as, that way you include everyone in your target market… Not just those who will sit through a short video.

The idea behind touch points stems from a strategy taught in the dating industry. One of the most effective things to do when you meet for the very first time is to move them around the bar, bookstore, etc., so that they see different backgrounds behind you. The intent is to make your date feel that they have been with you for a long time.

In marketing, touch points revolve around the same strategy. If you're filming videos for your prospects, change up the background and hit them through audio and text so that they feel they have been in your world for a long time, even though it may have only been a week or so. Constant contact is key, because it keeps your name in the back of that prospects mind. That's why these email marketing and banner retargeting are such great practices... They're easy to do and you can sustain them with pretty low effort.

There's no need to worry about setting all of this up right away, though. It will definitely be something to build upon throughout the process. Even then, it's not absolutely necessary, but it is a big bonus if you're able to do it. Not to mention you are going to be able to use these platforms to funnel visitors and prospects to your sales material, converting them into customers.

Remember, this guide is about creating and selling your digital product. What we have covered throughout the past few chapters is just focused on different angles that you can use to expose prospects to your brand... In other words, building awareness.

Never divert your focus away from your selling your product or service though. If you're creating a subpar product because you're too busy focusing a bunch of stuff that doesn't really matter, sales will be few and far between and you'll chalk up the product launch as a disaster.

Your offer is the most important thing you can think about.

Problem Seeking

The idea behind creating stuff to sell online is to solve a problem in a prospects life. The number one thing you need to look at when creating your product, is how much different your customer's life will be after utilizing your product.

The best offers are created because of a problem in the world that either needs solved.

Many business owners use examples of things they have overcome in their own lives as the basis for their businesses and the products/ services they sell. After all, if you are facing a problem, chances are there are others out there facing the same challenge in their lives.

So, creating products to help overcome your own problems often helps others solve theirs as well. Usually, those products are the most successful.

On the opposite side of the coin, if there's not a problem that is plaguing people, it's about time to start brainstorming a new offer. A problem definitely needs to exist if you want to make money helping people solve it. Teaching your customers that there's a problem only then to sell them something is a very big challenge and takes considerable resources.

If there is a problem, you need to ask yourself a few questions:

- Do I have a solution?

- What type of people are experiencing the problem?

- Is the problem emotionally based?

- Will my prospects spend money? (Which is a really big question!)

When analyzing these questions, if you find that your answer is a resounding no, move on.

Of those four questions, the last one is the most important though.

If people aren't going to spend their money, why bother investing time and resources in creating a product that probably won't sell!

The best product in the world isn't going to sell at all if it isn't a fixing a problem that doesn't plague enough people, or just plain isn't serious enough.

Here's how I know... The first product I created was a complete disaster.

When I began my career as an Internet marketer, I created an information product based on a blog post that I was getting a lot of traffic for. The product was a video series on creating slogans for businesses. I knew people had a problem with slogans. I was getting thousands of visitors a day to my blog post...

But after spending months recording videos, writing sales copy, writing emails and everything else that's required when launching a product... Nothing happened.

The bottom line was that people had a problem with creating slogans, but didn't want to spend money for a solution. It ended up with me abandoning the project after wasting close to a year on it, simply because it wasn't selling.

You may have a problem yourself, or maybe you see others with a specific problem you'd like to help them overcome.

Usually, creators have a story that binds them to the problem.

Maybe you have an employee that refuses to listen, or perhaps you've struggled with debt, or even became frustrated with your weight.

Your own take on the problem (and the subsequent solution) are what you are going to use to position this product to your prospects.

You have probably heard infomercials and ads on TV phrasing the problem that they help their customers solve...

- "I was once overweight but this is how I lost all that excess body fat."

- "I used to have problems with leading my team but then I found a new outlook on life."

- "I was struggling with too much debt – this is what I did to get out of it..."

Those transitions are techniques you can use to tell your story and then move into the actual sales pitch for the product.

If you can narrow down a worthwhile problem that needs solved, chances are there are thousands of people around the globe that will pay you for your solution.

You can't assume that everyone needs your product though, because they don't. Even if you believe your product is life changing, there are people out there who don't need it or simply aren't interested.

One thing to remember: **When you market to everyone, you market to no one.**

When creating your product and putting together your marketing and sales material, remember that there is only a percentage of the population who may suffer from the challenge that you're helping solve… You can't, and shouldn't try to, sell to everyone.

When you try to market a product that is aimed at everyone, you have to make the sales message so general that you aren't going to bond with your potential buyers, and they won't perceive your product as being special or worthwhile.

Drilling your target market down to a specific group of prospects is essential, especially when dealing with a really large niche. Think health and fitness. You can go after the general health and fitness segment with a product designed to "help people lose weight."

Or, you can go after a much more specific market in health and fitness targeting the people who are dieting to "lose the last ten pounds after they hit a plateau."

If you think that's drilling your market down to much, you'd be mistaken. First, your product is so specific, creating marketing material will be easy. And secondly, there are so many competitors in the health and fitness realm that it is essentially a "me too!"

situation. If you're able be a big voice in a small room, you'll get traction in the market.

Sure, you'll still have competitors, but you'll be able to use your product and your presence to make your offer the best in that niche.

I have seen very successful, very specific products that sell above and beyond because of how well they cater to a specific niche. Even further, within a niche, is a sub-niche, and within that a macro-niche, and so on and so forth. People read small-niche messages and feel included, thinking "Yup, that's me, he's talking to me." That's how a buyer's mind works, you just have to read into it.

Simplicity

The next step in creating a successful product is to make sure that the product offers a simple solution to a problem that your prospect knows that he or she has.

You want your product to offer quick implementations or thorough strategy that gets them closer to a solution in their life. Products that offer simple step-by-step solutions will always have higher adoption than those that contain complicated and convoluted strategies.

Buyers don't want a plan or list of long and difficult rules. They want a cut and dried, to-the-point blueprint of their plan. The best digital products end up being eBooks, video courses, and membership sites that help a customer implement solutions quickly and easily.

Examples of digital products that capitalize on simple strategies are:

- 4 simple steps to…

- 11 forgotten techniques to…

- 3 step formula to…

- 21 secret strategies for…

This material can be packaged up into reports, video series, audio products, webinars, and everything else in between. In fact, giving folks a simple tip that they can implement immediately with quick results will win a customer for life.

Now, the best way to break down complex topics is to establish simple stepping stones, where your reader can:

A. Visualize the end of the first step.

B. Accomplish that step.

C. Feel the success of the accomplishment (which you want to play up – the accomplishment!)

Think about this book. We've covered a lot already, and you've been exposed to countless strategies for finding niches, researching topics, naming customer avatars, and building out the first stages of your digital product.

In fact, this book is basically broken down into 8 sections.

1. Understanding digital products

2. Laying the foundation for a digital product

3. Understanding your target market

4. Generating leads

5. Product packaging

6. Website setup

7. Marketing and branding

By the time you're done with this book, you'll understand and be able to implement the steps needed to get your digital product created and up for sale.

If we started the book out with all the how-to training you needed to implement BEFORE we did a good job of explaining why you were doing what you were doing... You'd be lost by now.

So much of becoming a successful content creator is understanding the market and demographic of the people you are targeting and then creating for them!

Understanding your market and the potential customers is far more important than actually creating the product itself. That's why this book breaks the training down into smaller chunks that can be used now and referenced again later.

One thing I want to mention is that it is crucial to give your prospect or your new buyer a first success early on.

You want to give them that "aha" moment immediately before or after they buy your product. That feeling is what is going to hook them, and guarantees that they won't refund or feel buyer's remorse.

With all of the different technological advances in our society, attention span is decreasing rapidly. Online, you have about 4 seconds to grab the attention of a viewer. If you're unsuccessful, you've lost a potential customer.

When you are selling someone something that can be consumed immediately, like a video course, membership site, or eBook, you need to give your buyer a reason to feel good about his or her purchase. If they don't feel good about their purchase, you can bet they'll be returning it, and you're out that money, no matter how much you spent to acquire them as a customer.

In fact, I recently did a webinar promoting a $397 product. On the webinar I received two emails right after we were done that said "I actually got my first client within six minutes of doing what you told me to do. Before you even moved off that slide in the webinar, I got my first client."

You'd better believe they bought the course because they had their first success… That first "aha" moment.

In another course that I sold, that "aha" moment hit prospects in a free report they downloaded, even before they spent any money with me. In the report, I said "Without closing your browser, do this and you'll get your first lead."

The feedback helped me push my product and landed me more buyers for the course. Getting a customer a small success is EVERYTHING when it comes to buyer adoption.

How To Brainstorm

Before you hurt yourself trying to think of ways to write a book, figure out what to say in a video, or realize what type of information to put in a membership site; go back to what you learned in fourth grade and brainstorm!

In this section, we'll lay out some simple brainstorming techniques that serve as the foundation for every single one of the products we've ever sold. In fact, without doing this little exercise, I'd probably be pretty lost when it came to creating digital products...

Brainstorming the right way can make it easy to find the problem in your market, the solution and figuring out who you're going to sell it to.

Typically, I use a mind mapping software like MindJet's MindManager or MindMeister. Mindmeister has a free account and integrates with your iPad or iPhone so you can take the stuff with you.

At the center of the mind map I put the title, like How to Sell More Stuff Online. In fact, here's the mindmap I used to write this book:

Product Creation

- Niche Discovery
  - Skills and Talents
  - Goals and aspirations
  - current market
  - competition
  - research
  - presence
  - problem seeking
  - simple solutions
  - brainstorming
- Expanding Your Presence
  - Self vs. Traditional
  - Ebook vs. Print on Demand
  - Copyrights and Trademarks
  - Getting your book into book stores
  - Getting on Kindle and Ipad
  - Where to get help/finding a mentor
- Creating The Product
  - Ebook
  - Videos
  - Audio
  - Teleseminar
  - Workbook
  - Membership course
  - Association
- Marketing
  - Marketing to your growing list
  - Solo ads
  - Search engines
  - Affiliate marketing
  - Facebook
  - PPC
- Creating The Website
  - Squeeze page
  - Sale page
  - Thank you page
  - Download page
  - Membership site
  - Building the list
  - Content Promotion
- Sales Copy
  - Headline
  - Problem
  - Solution
  - Credibility
  - Product Info
  - Guarantee
  - Price
  - Close (logical/fear based)
  - Intensifiers

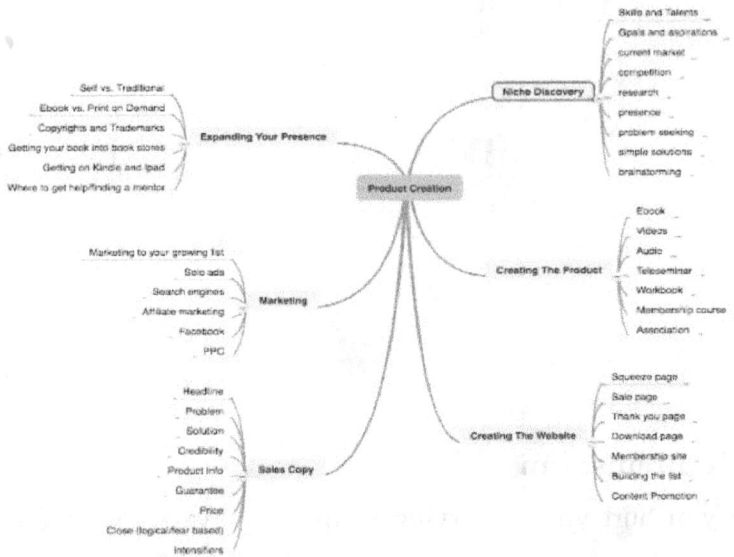

After giving the mindmap a title, "Product Creation," I started creating all of the different chapters from that center point.

Everything else related to the main topic goes next. Filtering at this stage isn't necessary because you can always go and take words and ideas out later.

Brainstorming at this stage allows you to get into the zone that your mind can play in and create complete outlines of books and courses. After brainstorming, you can concentrate fully on creating for one topic without having to worry about forgetting anything, because you've already created a map of where you need to be.

You can then immerse yourself in the thoughts and language for lengthy periods of time and get into the zone.

Thinking about content isn't essential at this point just yet. This activity in brainstorming will just serve as the basis for your course and the information that you'll be covering.

Much of the time, I'll write a bunch of words or topics that come to mind on the screen, just to get them out of my head. You can always go back and rearrange later.

Once everything is out of my head, I have the ability to get organized and separate those words and topics into categories, like chapters, so there is a good flow to it.

Creating the slides for content comes easily after that, because everything is pretty much laid out for you.

PART TWO: OFFERS

Creating Offers

There are a number of offers that I am going to teach you to create in this book - both high ticket and low ticket. An offer, very simply, is something that you sell online...

You make an offer. Your buyers spend money with you.

There are LOTS of different offers you can make, such as:

- Digital products

- Physical products

- Services

- Software

- Coaching

- Consulting

- Group-based programs

- And more...

The point of teaching the different types of offers is that there are multiple ways to make money online. Once you see how offers are created, you can go ahead and choose the types that match your skill set to make it easy for you.

For example, one of my client's skill sets positions her perfectly for doing what is known as a 'tele-seminar series.' A tele-seminar series, or webinar series, is a series of live sessions, calls or webinars relating to a niche. A 'Raw Foods Tele-seminar Series,' for example, might feature experts of preparing raw food, their nutrition, and dieting, with each topic being a separate call.

This client likes being on the ratio and phone. She's had the chance to interview hundreds of people already, and she's connected to others in her niche. She knows a lot of people that can help her create awareness for her brand. eBooks and video are foreign material to her though.

She has no idea how to create, edit, or stream video. For her, organizing a set of interviews around a given topic is a perfect match. The goal is to introduce you to multiple product types and let you choose your own so that you can create your product successfully.

Once you get the first digital product under your belt, there's a secret that I am going to introduce, and that's product testing. Product testing is a time-tested, smart strategy for setting everything up for your product before you actually create it... Meaning, you pre-sell your product and then deliver on the fly!

Now, offers are split up into "high ticket offers" and "low ticket offers." High ticket offers are the kind that require more of your personal time, which is extremely valuable. Then, there are low ticket offers (take this book for example) that don't require your time at all once it's done.

Normally, high ticket offers are considered to be $1,000 and above. Examples are:

- Coaching

- Consulting

- Masterminds

Low ticket offers are $999 or below, such as:

- eBooks

- Videos and video courses

- Audio and audio courses

- Tele-seminars and tele-seminar series.

- Workbooks

- Membership courses

- Associations

Each have their merits.

If you're looking to grow a big business with as little time required of you, you'll want to stick in the 'low ticket offers' realm... You'll have to sell a LOT of stuff to generate some serious revenue though.

How many copies of a $99 thing do you need to sell to make $1,000,000? The answer: 10,102!

If you don't mind spending your time helping clients and customers through coaching, consulting or masterminds... You can grow a lot faster because you'll need to sell fewer things.

To make a million dollars selling a $9,500 package, you need only sell 106 packages.

There is not right answer, but most of our clients end up doing a little bit of both to balance their scale and revenue. Not to mention, there are always those who will buy a book and then decide that they want you to do it for them...

In the following pages, you'll learn exactly how to set up each of these to make money, including the technology to use, the processes, the thinking and positioning and everything else that comes in between!

High Ticket vs. Low Ticket

Too many people try to build their businesses solely on selling low-priced products. That might work for huge corporations like McDonald's, but for small businesses, it can be devastating.

Simple math shows that you have to sell a lot more copies of a low-priced product to make a given amount of revenue. For example, 370 copies of a $27 product brings in about the same as just 20 sales of a $497 product.

Typically, almost all of those sales will be to new customers, which is where the cost of acquiring a customer comes into play. If you only sell low-priced products, you can't afford to spend much to get a new customer, at least not without losing money. That makes it hard to scale your business.

That's bad enough, but it gets worse. Many of these businesses have few or no other products available, so once they go to the trouble and expense to get a new customer, they have nothing else to sell to that person.

The solution to this problem is to develop a range of products and services in a variety of price ranges, what is commonly called a marketing funnel.

We'll get into more about how to do that later in this book. The key thing to remember right now is that you can do this, too. You don't have to create the entire funnel at once. You don't even have to know everything that will be in your funnel to get started creating it.

If you've only sold lower-priced products so far, you might be surprised to hear that creating high-ticket products and services is easier than you probably think it is. A lot of the difference is how you format and present your content and knowledge.

For example, the same content could be sold as a $25 book, made into a video training course priced at $197-$997, or taught at a $3000 live event.

In the upper range of the price scale, items in a funnel tend to be services rather than products. In many cases, the service consists mostly of helping people through the material and answering their questions. This type of service is fairly easy to create, as opposed to coming up with something completely different.

If you can write that $25 book, you're probably qualified to coach people on the same topic and could charge 10-20 times the price of the book for an hour of your time.

The main challenge for most people in this situation won't be doing the actual coaching. It will be convincing yourself that your service is worth the premium price and that you are "good enough" to coach people or perform other high-ticket services for them. (Hint: If you're knowledgable enough to write a book and you truly care about the client, you are good enough to coach them!)

Now, we are not telling you to avoid selling low-priced products. Those products have their place. Our point is to stress the importance of adding higher-priced offers to your funnel.

Two Ways to Sell High-Ticket Offers

If you haven't sold high-ticket offers before, you may be nervous about how to go about doing so. There are two main methods people use to do this.

The first strategy is to start by selling someone a low-priced product, then offering them the next highest-priced item in your funnel, and so on, working your way up the price scale. Some of this is done via upsells right after someone makes a purchase, and the rest is done by followup marketing to existing customers.

That is probably the most often-used strategy, since it seems logical that new customers would be more likely to buy the lower-priced items first. That is certainly the case with some customers, but not all of them.

The real danger of this sales strategy is that most of your customers never get exposed to your highest-priced products, because they haven't yet bought the products in the middle of your funnel.

Leading with Higher-Ticket Offers

We like the second strategy better. It's almost the direct opposite of the first one. You present your higher-priced offers first, then if the customer declines them, you offer them the lower-priced items. This gets your high-end offers in front of more people, faster.

Believe it or not, some people are more ready to buy your higher-priced stuff than your entry level items. Maybe they've already gone through your competitors' low priced products and are now looking for coaching, a more advanced (and higher priced) program, or someone to do the work for them. If all you're advertising to new people is your entry-level ebook, they will have no idea you even offer those other products and services, so they will look elsewhere for what they really want.

When it comes to selling those high-ticket items, especially to first-time customers, you do need to take a different approach to it. If you're used to using methods like Facebook or Google ads to send people directly to low-priced offers, you'll find that having ads like that go to high-ticket items doesn't work so well.

The Best Way to Make High-Ticket Sales

Here's what we've found works really well: strategy sessions. A strategy session is a short, free, one-on-one call between you and the prospect. An average call lasts 15-30 minutes. It's not a sales call, although sometimes it will result in a sale. The main purpose is to see if the prospect and your product or service are a good fit for each other.

As much as you might want everyone to buy, eventually you'll realize that's not ideal. Some of the people you talk with won't be a good fit. Your offer might be too advanced or too basic for where they are right now. They might have goals that don't align with what you offer. Or in the case of something like coaching, there might be a personality conflict.

Trust me, sometimes politely telling the prospect you're not the right person to help them is the best thing for both of you. Otherwise there is a risk of selling to someone with unrealistic expectations or who won't take any action or won't get along with you, and none of those are good things.

The phrase *strategy session* comes from the world of coaching, though the concept works well with almost any high-ticket offer, especially services.

In our second book, *Convert*, we talk extensively about Strategy Sessions; how to set them up, how to promote them, and how to close the sale. I don't want to hijack this conversation here, but know that the resource is available when you want to get into selling higher ticket offers!

The Benefits of Premium Pricing

Making more revenue per sale is just one benefit of adding higher-ticket offers to your marketing funnel.

Here are a few more:

- You can help people much more by selling them a higher-ticket service that allows you to spend time with them than you ever can from putting all your knowledge into a product like a book.

- High-ticket offers tend to attract higher-quality customers and clients. Many business owners have noticed that their higher-paying clients are usually easier to work with and generate fewer support issues than people who buy low-priced products.

- Those clients are also much more likely to take action because of the investment they have made with you. That makes them likelier to get the results they seek, which means happy clients.

- When you sell higher-priced services and deliver quality, you can expect referrals. Many service providers get so much business from referrals that they no longer need to advertise their services since they are fully booked.

- You're more likely to get testimonials from clients or students you have worked with personally (i.e. higher-paying clients) than from low-ticket buyers.

- You'll get known as an expert in your niche as a result of offering higher-ticket services and products. Some of that is a result of the increased testimonials and referrals, but some is just a result of having higher-ticket offers. Many people who see those offers, even if they don't purchase them, will think of you as an expert.

  Being recognized as an expert leads to being invited to guest on webinars and podcasts, to speak at events, to do media interviews, and other opportunities that will make you more famous.

- If your funnel has higher-ticket offerings in it, it's much easier to attract quality affiliates. They will seek you out rather than you having to chase them.

- If you give good service and build your funnel intelligently, some of your clients will continue to work with you for long periods of time. It's much easier to continue working with a happy client than to recruit a new one.

- You'll find that you're happier with your business and your life as a result of all these things.

The Benefits of Low Ticket Pricing

Low ticket offers, those below $1,000 in price, also give you a lot of advantages depending on what you want your business to do for you.

- You won't be stuck in the "time = money" trap. Every sale that comes in won't be dependent on your time or you needing to personally fulfill something. If someone buys a book or a digital course, they get it or get access to it and that's it.

- Low ticket pricing requires less coaxing to sell. Oftentimes, the sales come from sales videos, webinars, sales pages or shopping carts. Folks figure out what they want and buy it. High ticket offers need more personal support and interaction from you or your sales staff, especially when you're getting started.

- You'll stop wasting time on tire-kickers. As we said, Strategy Sessions are great ways to sell high ticket offers, but what if the prospect isn't qualified? You've just wasted an hour or more on the phone and you're not getting the sale. With lower end offers, they either buy or they don't. It's as simple as that.

- For lower end products, especially digital, the thing you're fulfilling is access. You can't force anyone to go through a course or read a book, and the majority won't... It's hard to believe, but it's true. What you're selling them is access to the material, software, training or videos. Once they've got their access, then the product is fulfilled.

- Low ticket offers qualify buyers. Buyers, people who are willing and able to spend money with you, are worth 7 to 12 TIMES more money to you. By selling a lower priced offer first, you're qualifying buyers more quickly and can then march them through an upsell path.

At the end of the day though, you need to ask yourself what you're willing to give up to generate revenue. If it's time, then high ticket offers are for you. If it's a longer growth period (before you hit the big numbers), it's low ticket offers.

If, however, you want both… Like most of our clients… Then you can take the best of low ticket offers and high ticket offers and combine them into the same sales funnel!

Models for High-Ticket Offers

The high-ticket offers you can put together are limited only by your imagination and talent. Here are five types of packages to get you started.

One-on-One: These are offers that require your personal time, such as one-on-one coaching, tutoring, mentoring, etc.. That time is the primary reason for the higher price, since you have an absolute limit on how many hours you can give to your clients.

Assisted One-on-One: This is an offer which includes some high-value elements in addition to one-on-one time. The idea is to design them to reduce the amount of one-on-one time required, while still maintaining the value of the package.

One common element is prerecorded training. For example, if you already sell a video course, you could include that with your coaching package. That will save you from having to teach the entire course individually to each student. It will also increase the value of the package, since clients will have the course to refer back to after the coaching has ended.

If you don't already have a course, you can record training videos or create other material for your students to go through to supplement the coaching. That way the students can learn much of what they need from the prerecorded training, and your one-on-one sessions can focus on questions and advanced topics.

Hint: Notes from a coaching program are a great foundation for creating a related course, if you don't already have one. Include case studies and testimonials from your successful students, with their permission, of course.

Assisted Group: Many coaches offer group coaching as a lower-priced option in their funnel. Since they can have several students in the same session, they can charge less per student.

With some thought put into designing these packages, you can position an Assisted Group package to be as valuable as a one-on-one offer.

One key to doing this is to keep the group small. (Putting 50 people on a webinar is not group coaching!) In a small group setting, students can learn from the questions asked by other students. Being in a group also takes the pressure off a student to feel like they have to maintain half the conversation, like they might feel in a one-on-one situation.

Another key, if you have enough students, is to divide them into groups by skill level, interest, or some other major factor, so that the discussion is more targeted and relevant to them. For example, if your general niche is parenting, you might find out that several students have babies and toddlers, while others have just school-age kids. It would make sense to separate the students by the age group of their kids, so you can make the discussions more suitable for everyone.

High-End Products: Although many high-ticket offers are services, let's not forget about products. Common examples of high-ticket products are courses, seminars, workshops, bootcamps, and other types of training, as well as software. These can be delivered in many different formats: physical or online products, live in-person events, live online events such as webinars, or various combinations of these.

If you're selling high-ticket services, there are almost certainly some products you could create which would be a logical fit for your business.

Masterminds: Some of the highest-ticket offers of all are masterminds. A mastermind is a group of people who get together to discuss and work on a common interest, such as a specific type of business. For our purposes, the ideal candidates for a mastermind would be people who have taken our course on a particular subject and/or are in our coaching program.

In a properly-designed mastermind, students learn from each other as well as from the group leader. People join masterminds to get access to the other students as much as to learn from the leader. Many business deals and partnerships have started between people who met in masterminds.

There are many ways to structure a mastermind. Some of them are one-time events, like a weekend retreat. Others are ongoing; students meet online or offline on a regular basis such as weekly or monthly. For ongoing masterminds, students typically commit to participating for a long period of time, such as a year, to keep consistency in a group.

Examples of High-Ticket Packages You Can Create

There are many types of high-ticket one-on-one offers you can put together. Here are some ideas to get you started.

Monthly: This is a great way to start if you're new to high-ticket offers and for your new clients, since the time commitment is short. Your monthly package could consist of a one-hour call per week with the client, possibly with some email access to you between the calls. If you both want to continue working together at the end, the client can renew for another month.

You should insist that all the calls are scheduled in advance and that the client shows up on time. The best way to schedule is to stick with the same time and day of the week for each call for a given client.

For best results, structure the calls rather than just getting on the phone and chatting. Here is a typical format for coaching:

- What action did the student take since your last call? Were all goals for the week achieved?

- What questions or problems does the student have?

- Training and discussion of what to do next.

- Set goals for the coming week.

The first and last steps should just take a few minutes, with the middle two taking up the bulk of the time.

This format is a good way to keep students on track and accountable, since they will realize they have to tell you if they took action or not, and why any goals weren't met.

Quarterly / Semiannual / Annual: These are the same as the Monthly package, except for the duration. Give people a discount for making a longer time commitment and paying in advance. For an annual package you might charge 9-10 times the monthly rate.

If you're new to this, you might want to start with just monthly and quarterly packages until you get more experience delivering your services.

Live Events: There are many ways to structure live events, from a one-day workshop to a week-long bootcamp. One of the most lucrative is a one-on-one, in-person meeting with the client. You can travel to them, or they can come to you. This type of meeting typically lasts a day.

Premium One-on-One: This package could include elements like more access to you, more one-on-one coaching, extra services, or other perks not included in your basic package.

Done-for-You Services: Another type of high-end services is a whole category known as done-for-you. Instead of teaching your clients how to do something, or coaching them through it, you just do it for them. Many people would rather just pay an expert to do the task for them than go to the trouble of doing it themselves.

Continuity: This is any service or product that is billed on a recurring basis. Some examples of continuity are access to a membership site or software, services like consulting or coaching (when recurring billing is in effect). Although continuity isn't automatically high-ticket, we mention it here because including it in your business model can really help your bottom line. A continuity program adds a fairly predictable, steady income stream to your bottom line.

The Bridged Offer Model

When you start planning your high-ticket services and products, think strategically. Design them so there is a logical flow from one to the next. Figure out good reasons why your clients or customers would go from one package to the next.

For example, at the low end of the funnel, it makes sense why someone would move from a $27 ebook to a $197 video course, even if both contain basically the same information. Videos have higher perceived value than text-based content.

It's easier to teach some things in a video than in a book, because you can show people visually how to do things. Think of the difference between a recipe in a book and a chef on TV showing how to prepare the same dish.

On the higher end of the funnel, it makes sense that someone would upgrade from a group coaching program to one-on-one coaching or from coaching to a mastermind or a done-for-you service.

Although we often use coaching as an example, please keep in mind that your high-ticket service could be something completely different. Coaching isn't suitable for every niche, and some people prefer not to do coaching.

That's fine. Just think about which services and products would make sense for you and your clients or customers.

Don't forget the power of strategy sessions. They are a great way to bring people into almost any high-ticket service and to research your niche.

Finally, try to think of at least one continuity program you can add to your funnel.

If you'd like some help figuring out what this sales funnel would look like, make sure to book a call with us here:

http://doneforyou.com/schedule/

Coaching

From an offer standpoint, I tend to think of coaching and consulting as two different disciplines. In the last few years, coaching has exploded as "Life Coaches" and "Professional Coaches" have become more mainstream, but there is still a great deal of opportunity when you have your own tribe..

The International Coaching Federation defines coaching as partnering with clients in a thought-provoking and creative process that inspires them to maximize their personal and professional potential, which is particularly important in today's uncertain and complex environment. Coaches honor the client as the expert in his or her life and work and believe every client is creative, resourceful and whole. Standing on this foundation, the coach's responsibility is to:

- Discover, clarify, and align with what the client wants to achieve

- Encourage client self-discovery

- Elicit client-generated solutions and strategies

- Hold the client responsible and accountable

As such, as a coach your role is to help your client achieve the results they're after.

Now, those results could be in business, health, finances... You name it. If there is someone who could benefit from your experience and could be held accountable by you, then there's an opportunity for a coaching program.

As we've already discussed, there are lots of ways to create a coaching program where you are at the center OR where something you create is at the center of the program (like a book or course) and your role is to help your client through it.

The two things you really need to be a coach are:

- Experience from your own life or because of a certification or training program

- The ability to encourage and motivate your clients to do the things they must to do get a result.

Now, I know you're probably thinking that it needs to be more complicated than that... It doesn't.

As an example, think about an NFL coach. They didn't go to school to coach football. They might have gone to school for something related, but there isn't a degree in "Coaching football."

Most likely, they started coaching high school freshmen. When the JV coach moved on, they were pulled up and coached sophomores for a few seasons. From there, they were hired as the Offensive

Coordinator for the Varsity team… They did a great job and got the promotion to head coach when their predecessor retired.

… From there, their winning percentage got them appointed to the helm of the local college.. Then a Division 1 team came knocking. And finally, they graduated to being a coach in the NFL.

What got them to the NFL was their experience and their talent.

You, my friend, have what it takes to be a coach, if you want to be. As we've talked about in the entire first section of this book, you've got incredible skills and talents. If coaching makes sense for the life you want to live, then so be it.

As you can expect, coaching requires a lot of talking and being on the phone. Some coaches do most of their work through email but they're few and far between.

Types Of Coaching

There are literally as many types of coaches as you can think of…

You don't have to be local with your clients. In fact, you can have clients all over the world and engage with them through Skype or on the phone… So really, you can be 'placeless' if you'd like. They won't mind!

Here are some types of coaches that we've worked with through our DoneForYou.com programs:

- Business development coaches

- Life coaches

- Speaking coaches

- Fitness and Weight Loss coaches

- Spiritual Coaches

- Breathing Coaches

- Financial Coaches

- Happiness Coaches

- Dating Coaches

You name it, we've helped them put together and sell a coaching program…

What To Expect As A Coach

To be sure, coaching is trading time for money BUT you can make a lot of money doing it. You can also give tremendous value to your clients and make a real impact in their lives and businesses.

Here are some things you can expect:

- You will always be on call. If you have 10 clients who are each given 1 hour a week on the phone and unlimited email support, your work week will be full. If each of those clients is paying $2,500 a month, it's probably worth it though.

- It's hard to scale coaching without hiring or outsourcing. Because time is limited and there are only so many hours, you'll find yourself hitting a natural ceiling when it comes to growing your business.

- You will most likely be covering the same material with your clients at the same time, so it'll feel like you're repeating yourself a lot. It's often beneficial to structure some of that material in a digital course which we'll be covering in a later chapter.

- The best way to sell coaching is on a webinar where the call to action is a "Strategy Session." (We cover this exact process in the second book of the series, *Convert*.)

How To Price Coaching

Unfortunately, there is no correct answer when it comes to the right price for coaching.

- You want it to have value for your client.

- You want the coaching to be something they will invest in month after month.

- You want to make sure that their investment is outweighed by what they're gaining as a result of your coaching.

I've talked to hundreds of coaches over the years. Some, I think are too cheap. They don't value their time enough to charge what they're worth. And, in those cases, it's sometimes not worthwhile to be a coach because they aren't making enough money!

Often, when I think about coaching, I think of it as a highly valued, top dollar offer… Meaning, if you're going to give someone your time and attention, you need to be paid well for it.

Usually that means charging no less than $1,000 a month for your services.

Here are some common pricing and offer structures I employ or suggest for our clients:

- $2,500 for 2 60-minute coaching sessions per month with unlimited email support. Multi-month discounts are applicable.

- $4,000 for 4 60-minute coaching sessions per month with unlimited email support and "Done for you" elements. Multi-month discounts are applicable.

- $1,997 for 8 weeks of coaching with a companion digital product that does most of the heavy lifting in teaching a client.

The thing that works for you might not work for someone else, but you want to balance the investment you command from clients with what you're giving up to get it… Time.

How To Fulfill Coaching

Coaching is usually fulfilled through:

- **In-Person Conversations.** That might be on the phone, Skype calls, Zoom Conferences or face to face. You really only need access to a phone or computer to successfully coach your clients.

- **Email.** Outside of your normally scheduled calls, you'll probably get emails pretty regularly from your clients. It's wise to make sure to answer quickly, preferable the same day.

- **Text messages and Facebook Messages.** Since we're always connected in one way or another, clients tend to send messages using the communication medium that they're most used to or the one they're using when they have a thought… Any thought! So, expect to get text messages on a Saturday or FB messages in the middle of the night.

Consulting

Consulting is often thought of as coaching, and some of the elements of coaching might be consultative in nature; but they're not the same.

Consulting is defined as the business of giving expert advice to other professionals, typically in financial and business matters.

One of the primary differences is how consulting is billed for.

Consulting is typically project based, meaning the deliverables are clearly defined and center around one area of expertise. You may do a little 'coaching,' as in you're making sure things are getting done… But that isn't your only responsibility.

You're evaluating, assessing, and offering guidance for a specific thing.

One way I personally think about it is coaching is when you're helping one person or one organization achieve their goals and your primary responsibility is accountability and encouragement.

Consulting, however, is when you're working with an organization on a project and leveraging your experience to better a process they already have in place.

How Deals Are Done

Consulting deals are usually pitched through a proposal.

You'll need to:

- Have at least one conversation with your prospective client and figure out exactly what they need help with and whether or not that corresponds to a skillset you possess.

- Understand the scope of the project, including what they need done and what it's going to require from you.

- Take into consideration what they have access to and what else they'll need to complete the project successfully, including an approximation of the time you'll need to invest in the project.

- You'll then write up and send a proposal breaking down all of those elements into a deal. You'll be paid an hourly rate for your contribution. So, if you'll be working on a project for approximately 100 hours over the course of 6 months, and you typically charge $200 an hour, you'll be paid $20,000.

- After the proposal is sent, you might have a few more conversations and then the deal will close. After you get paid, you get to work!

Consultative Pricing

Consulting deals are normally billed hourly and for an approximation of the time you'll spend on the project... Your range can be anywhere from $50 an hour to $1000 an hour - more if you're in high demand!

There are a few things you'll want to take into consideration:

- You're paying your own overhead, so make sure that's reflected in your pricing.

- Some skillsets are in more demand than others. The higher the demand on the skillset, the more money you should charge.

- If you're the best in your industry, you can charge a premium. I know Internet marketers who charge $5,000 an hour and SAAS software server admins who are at $1,500 an hour. It's all dependent on how much you feel you're worth and how much your clients will pay.

The goal for you should be to secure a contract that'll get you paid well both now and into the future!

Software

My favorite type of offer to create these days is software. This is very much a personal preference, partly because I have a degree in MIS (Management of Information Systems) and partly because I was always fascinated by what a computer could do for you...

The software we create helps you do sales, marketing and business-related things faster than doing stuff manually...

We have software for:

- Curating and writing blog posts (curately.org)

- Writing email marketing sequences, video sales letters, webinars and building marketing pages (scriptly.org)

- Sending out email to your list (convertly.org)

- Tracking effectiveness and conversion of your website (statly.org)

- Creating surveys and quizzes for your customers and prospects (askly.org)

- Scheduling sales calls and strategy sessions (timeslots.org)

Each of those software tools solves a problem that I used to have or that my clients have… That was the inspiration for it.

At the end of the day, we build stuff to make work seem less like work.

Your software application might be different. You might have an idea for something on a mobile device or a downloadable program that sits on a customer's desktop… My point is, as long as your software solves a problem for your customers, it's relatively easy to sell. Creating it though, is a different story.

Building Software

I have a programming background. I used to be able to code, but I don't anymore. I choose not to. For me, I try to stay far enough away from the software to be able to sell it well.

Here's my process for creating and selling software:

1. **Start with the problem you're going to solve.** Figure out a way, however crude, for software to make someone's life easier. You don't need a fully fleshed out idea, but an idea of how you'd want it to work.

2. **Draw up the screens of the software.** If you have an iPad and a stylus, you can draw it there. A piece of paper and a

pen will work too. What you want to design is the screens that your customers will interact with.

3. **Once you have your screens drawn, post the job on upwork.com,** which is an outsourced job portal. There are thousands of programmers who can build your project there and they'll start bidding on the job.

4. **Pick a coder who's middle of the road price wise.** You don't want to pick the cheapest or the most expensive. Look at their past jobs, feedback and portfolio to find someone that seems like they'll work.

5. **Award the job and send them your screen drawings.** I usually record a quick Camtasia or Screenflow video walking them through the page designs so that they know how the screens relate to one another.

6. **Have them start building, sending you weekly check-ins or status updates to report on their work.** Upwork also has a nifty screen grabbing function that shows you the hours that you're paying them for and the work that they're doing.

7. **Have them deploy your software to your web server**, and test it out!

8. **Once it's ready, start getting beta testers** in to 'break it…'

9. **Then start selling!**

TimeSlots.org, my first software application, took 5 months to build. Scriptly.org, the second app, took just 6 weeks because the programmer could re-use chunks of code for the new project. Not to mention, we had been working together for 6 or so months so we knew what each other was expecting.

What To Know About Software

There are some things you need to be prepared for when building and selling software…

- **Your programmer isn't a sales and marketing guy.** He/ She won't know when it's ready to sell. Once you have a MVP (Minimum Viable Product) that you can start selling, you need to pull the trigger. Your programmer is just responsible for making it run.

- **Software is expensive - probably the most expensive of all of the offer types in this book.** Your startup costs will range between $10,000 and $25,000 depending on programmers skill level and your working relationship with them. Don't go for a big programming team. Just find one person who can get it off the ground for you.

- **It'll take a while to hit MVP status.** My first hosted software app took 5 months to launch. My second app took 6 months. The third app, 5 months. The fourth, 11 months. There is very little you can do when someone else is programming to control timelines, other than hiring additional programmers. Some software applications take weeks to build. Some take years.

- **Once your software is live, you still need marketing!** Even after everything is up and live, you still need a website, sales copy, a way to charge subscribers, etc.

- **The simpler the application, the better it'll do.** With software, remove as many steps as possible to streamline the onboarding process. Make it easy to use while still solving the problem you originally set out to conquer!

- **For hosted software applications, think recurring revenue.** The name of the game with software is recurring revenue. You'll probably need to give away free trials to start, but the goal is to get most of those people to stay with you for months and years!

- **Consultative Sales Calls are the money-maker.** Software applications that use a sales team make far and away more money than any other model. It's more complex than posting and app in the App Store or putting up a "Subscribe Now" button, but it'll keep the bell ringing!

(Now, I realize this isn't an exhaustive manual on building software, but if you'd like a hand in brainstorming or thinking about software, make sure to schedule a call with me at: **http://doneforyou.com/schedule**)

Physical Products

Business and industry was built on selling physical products to customers. Before 5 years ago or so, it was much more difficult.

To sell physical products, you would have needed to have an idea, prototype it, manufacture it, secure inventory, find customers and ship that inventory to them…

It was a LOT more difficult and required a lot more capital than it does now.

Now, anyone has access to physical products and can sell through the largest eCommerce platform on the planet, amazon.com, with a few clicks of a mouse. Or, you can create your own store and be live in minutes with shopify.com!

If you don't want to fulfill the products (as in pick, pack and ship), Amazon has a service for that too… It's called Amazon FBA. You can learn more about it at:

https://services.amazon.com/fulfillment-by-amazon/

In fact, in terms of business models, physical products are one of the best (and fastest) ones to start! Physical products also tend to have a better conversion rate online because customers actually receive something in the mail!

Being Vertical Specific

At the beginning of this book, we talked about skills and talents and all the things you bring to the table in your business. One thing I need to mention, especially with physical products, is the fact that you need to grow your brand in a particular vertical.

For instance, if you're selling health and fitness products, you should be specific about the products you have in your product line.

You don't want to sell one type of yoga mat, coupled with muscle building supplements, and workout equipment.

What you do want to do is find a high quality yoga mats in different colors, textures and thicknesses; paired with mat towels and clothing.

With physical products, building your brand is of paramount importance. Your buyers will be back to buy more stuff AND they'll tell their friends about your company!

Not to mention, they'll share your links on their social profiles and review your products online.

Sourcing Physical Products

It used to be that you needed an idea to sell physical products. You had to do something better or different without infringing on patents, get it prototyped and produced, and then you'd be up and running.

Now, finding physical products is as simple as going to alibaba.com.

Alibaba is a Chinese website where manufacturers list all of the products that they produce for wholesale purchase. You can also buy individual items but that doesn't make much sense if you plan on selling a lot of stuff!

In fact, a simple search of Alibaba yields 265,000+ products (yoga mat types) that can sell!

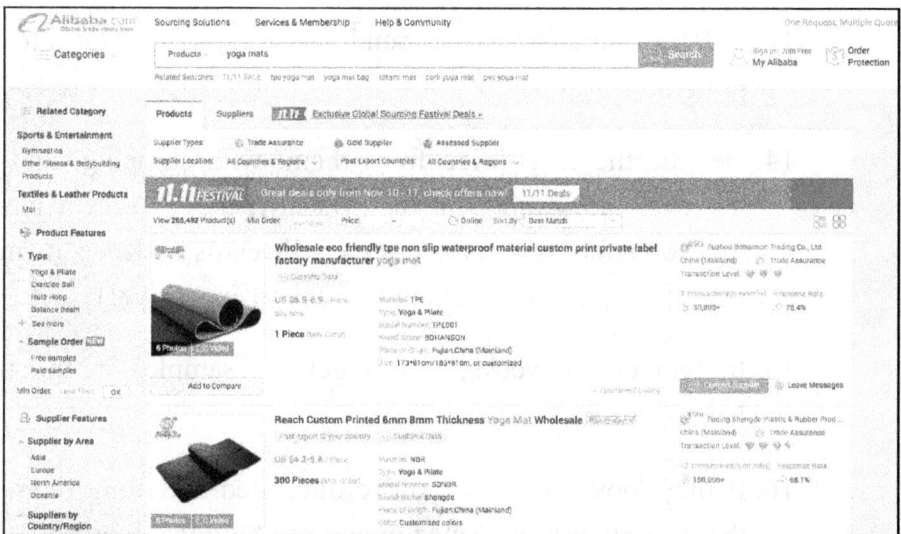

That's a LOT of possibility!

Now, consider that there are hundreds of thousands of types of products ready and waiting for you on Alibaba! All you have to do is find something you want to sell and contact the manufacturer!

Getting Started With Physical Products

There are lots of best practices to selling physical products... Books and books have been and will be written on the subject. Here's the condensed version of starting up though:

10. Put together a list of products you are interested in selling.

11. Source those products on Alibaba, saving the links to a spreadsheet.

12. Choose 4 or 5 of those products and message the manufacturer. Oftentimes, you'll hear back within a day but there is sometimes a language barrier so be mindful of that.

13. Ask the manufacturer to send you a sample of the product, preferably 2 or 3.

14. Get the the total price from them, with shipping, and pay however they want you to. Usually, they'll accept paypal, wire transfer, and sometimes credit cards. (Keep in mind, this is shipping from China - it will be expensive!)

15. In two or so weeks, you'll get the samples in the mail. Inspect them.

16. If they look good and you're interested in selling them, list them in Shopify or Amazon and see how fast they sell. You may need to run some of your own ads for the promotion.

17. When you sell through, pause your listing and order in bulk from the Chinese manufacturer. They usually have a minimum order quantity specific to their company.

18. Pay for the inventory and shipping and re-enable the listing!

It's an easy process. Just keep in mind you are importing these goods. It'll take time to get to the states.

If you'd rather source to a manufacturer stateside, that's great too. You'll get better shipping rates and won't have to worry about imports, but the material cost will be higher.

Your List Is STILL Your Biggest Asset

Even if you're selling physical products, you're email list is still one of your biggest assets. Those buyers will be back. The prospects who haven't purchased yet - they still need to hear from you.

Your list will be your single best source of revenue-driving traffic in your business as long as you keep up with them.

Not to mention, when you want to launch something new (or are thinking about adding a product to your lineup), they're great to ask before you plop down a big pile of cash for inventory.

In fact, with your email list, you may even pre-sell your inventory! You just need to make sure your customers know they won't be getting their stuff for a few weeks.

Mastermind Groups

A "Mastermind Group" was defined in Napoleon Hill's book, "Think And Grow Rich," as:

> "The coordination of knowledge and effort of two or more people, who work toward a definite purpose, in the spirit of harmony."

TheSuccessAlliance.com writes that Mastermind Groups offer a combination of brainstorming, education, peer accountability and support in a group setting to sharpen your business and personal skills. A Mastermind Group helps you and your mastermind group members achieve success. Participants challenge each other to set powerful goals, and more importantly, to accomplish them.

What's more, Mastermind Groups can be incredible revenue drivers for the people who put them together.

The goal of a group is always to being people together. Sometimes, the groups are diverse in nature, pulling in people with different experiences, backgrounds, skillsets and the like to share knowledge.

Other times, the group is industry specific or specific to a cause or outcome.

… The best ones offering accountability, knowledge transfer and guidance.

Now, there are lots of ways a Mastermind Group can be run. That's something specific to the organizer's intentions. Some are in-person. Some are online. Some are expensive. Some are quite cheap of free.

Usually though, the person who puts the Mastermind together is well networked and reserves the mastermind for their absolute best customers, acquaintances or friends.

Types of Masterminds

As you an imagine, there are LOTS of ways to run a Mastermind. It can be:

- **Online**, where all members get access to a forum, membership site or Facebook Group where the can check in, support other members, and share what they're doing or what they learned. There are also usually calls or digital webinars scheduled to teach members something new. Online-only masterminds tend to be between $200 and $300 a month to join.

- **Offline**, where all members gather in person once a month or so over a meal. These groups tend to be smaller because of physical limitations but the relationships tend to be better. In small, personal groups your Mastermind Members will get to know each of the members more deeply. Offline Mastermind

Groups range from being free to being thousands a month. There is not hard and fast rule.

- **Mixed**, where the majority of the interaction is digital but there are a few physical meet ups throughout the year. These tend to be the most expensive, sometimes ranging from $1,000 a month to $100,000 a year. The digital portion of the membership is made up of a Facebook Group or forum and webinars, while the physical meet ups tend to coincide with industry events. The group will meet a a few days before or after the event.

At the end of the day, the group needs to help each other advance their lives in one way or another, by offering support, education and accountability!

Getting Mastermind Members

When you first start your Mastermind Group, you'll usually have to work to get members... Your first members might be your best clients or customers, friends, acquaintances and the like.

Sometimes to get people into a group, they need to know that there are other people already in it and receiving value for being a part of it.

For Offline, In-Person Masterminds, the magic number of group members is seven. I know, that doesn't seem like many. Too many more than that and relationships will lose their focus. Too many fewer and the group won't running at full steam.

For Online or Mixed Masterminds, there really isn't a maximum number of members you should have. Some of the best Mixed

Masterminds have thousands of members and their tribe is as connected as they would be if it was a smaller group.

The trick to getting and keeping Mastermind Members is to figure out how it works with the rest of your business.

As I said earlier, most Mastermind Leaders have products and services that they offer to the general public. Their best customers, people who are open and willing to be part of a group, tend to be the ones who are invited.

In short, they use it as an upsell model.

- They might have a book selling for $19 on Amazon.

- Then, they sell a digital course on their website for $299.

- From there, they offer services ranging from $1,000 to $10,000

- And for the best customers, they offer a Mastermind Group filled with their best students, clients and friends for $5,000 a year.

In exchange for the $5,000, they get access to the entire Mastermind Group online or in person, plus accountability calls, check-ins and education that will help them move their business or life forward in some way.

Events

If you're into public speaking, then you might consider running events for your tribe, either locally or nationally.

Now, when I say, "Events," I'm referring to anything you do where you put a group of people in a room and teach them something. There are lots of terms used for events, such as:

- Workshops

- Retreats

- Conferences

- Lunch & Learn's

- Summits

For all intents and purposes, it doesn't matter what you call it or how big it is. You might get 5 people in a room and call it a workshop… Or take 20 people to some destination and a multi-day retreat… Or, do a full-blown conference where you have 600 people in attendance…

The trick is in figuring out how you are going to monetize the event.

Getting Attendees

For the most part, attendees are going to show up because they want to learn something or be a part of something. There's something in their life which is posing a challenge for them or there's something happening that they want to be prepared for.

On the other side of that coin, your event is something they don't want to miss out on.

Your content should be centered around a problem that they're experiencing. The solution to that problem will take shape in the form of talks or presentations.

The thing you have to remember though is your attendees need to be uncomfortable enough that they are willing to attend.

There are a lot of costs associated with going to an event.

- They need to arrange travel and lodging if it isn't local.

- They will probably need to take time off of work or get their boss to approve...

- They'll be away from their desk, their house, and/or their families.

Today, with webinars and digital tools like Skype or Zoom, it's sometimes much easier to just attend digitally. You need to give them a reason to show up.

Event-Based Revenue Models

There are three ways you can make money from an event. No one way is the best way, either. You have to consider how your business is (will be) set up and figure out how events will fit into the mix.

- **Charge for tickets.** If you're charing an admission fee, that'll be the first barrier of entry for registrants. You want to make sure that the ticket price is affordable while still taking event costs into consideration.

- **Free admission with in-room sales opportunities.** If you're allowing free admission, your no-show rate will be higher and you aren't making anything at the door, BUT you can offer products or services to a captivated audience in person…

- **Tickets and pitches.** This is the most prevalent option. Normally, event organizers will charge a small admission fee, sometimes just $1, because it encourages attendees to show. Then, at the end of the event, they'll make an offer to everyone in attendance that will make up the cost of the event itself.

Typically, your ticket sales will not cover the cost of the event on it's own, unless you're charging quite a bit per ticket… By quite a bit, I mean $500 and up. For attendees to pay that, you need to make sure you have some great speakers!

Costs Associated With Events

The first time I put on an event, I will admit that I was surprised by how much it cost. We rented a room in a hotel in San Diego for 3 days and didn't come close to breaking even. Some of the things I learned were:

- **Food and Beverage (F&B) is expensive.** Oftentimes, a hotel will be reasonable on the price of the room but the only way for you to get it is to sign an F&B contract where they cater for you. This can get quite costly.

- **Audio/Video.** Each hotel has A/V people you can contract and every service you add adds to the price…

- **Room Setup.** Usually, the room setup is free. If the hotel has to move tables around, they'll charge you extra.

- **Decoration.** Linens, drapery, and lights are all extra. If you want to room to look perfect, you'll be paying for it.

Don't go big for the first event you run. Get your feet wet and learn the ins and outs of the event business, including what's going to work with your audience first, before signing the big hotel room contract.

Starting Small

If events are your ticket (pun intended), start small. It'll save you a lot of money and even more headaches than jumping right into the deep end first.

1. Do a local event. Your attendees can and will come to you if you give them enough time to plan and prepare.

2. Find a room that doesn't have catering costs. This can be an executive suite at a hotel (with a table), a library, a

conference space at your local Chamber of Commerce, or a beautiful house you rent off of HomeAway.com.

3. Feed your guests for anything longer than half a day. Since a hotel won't be catering, make sure to plan meals and breaks for them. If there are no nearby restaurants, cook! Or organize travel to get them fed (ie. Uber SUVs).

4. Plan out exceptional content for them!

One of the best event models I know is from a guy by the name of Kevin Nations. He teaches a course called, "Big Money, Small Events."

The entire training is about monetizing small, five to seven person events through ticket sales and course/mastermind upsells. He doesn't use fancy conference spaces either… Oftentimes, he'll just invite people to his house!

eBook & Book Creation

The first type of digital product we will introduce is about the simplest form, eBooks! If you don't know what an eBook is, you're probably an alien, but let's go through it anyway.

eBooks are digital copies of books, delivered in either device specific formats, like Kindle/iBooks, or as PDF files that are readable in Adobe reader, which is installed on 98% of all computers. Now, web browsers will open up a PDF natively, so there's almost never anything to install for your buyers.

With the success of tablet devices and mobile phones, eBooks have really become mainstream.

eBooks are the easiest digital information product in the world to create. They're also brilliant for lead generation, meaning you can give them away to collect email addresses pretty easily. There are a few different types of eBooks you should know about – mostly based on how long they are.

First though, let's talk about how to put them together.

eBook Structure

Typically, I structure an eBook this:

- **Cover Page** - Create a graphical cover page with the name of your eBook, colors, etc. I've used CoverActionPro for years and it's served me well. You can also have a designer on Elance do it for you.

- **Table of Contents** - I'm sure you're familiar with a table of contents page, but it normally goes next. The only difference is that this table of contents actually links to certain sections of the book. Normally, if you create your eBook in Microsoft Word or Pages for Mac, it'll create the links in the exported PDF.

- **Bio or 'Who Am I' Page** - I generally include a bio or short page about me and why what they're about to read is relevant to their situation. This is also a good time to reinforce their buying decision and tell them that they made a good choice!

- **The Problem** - The fourth section is where you actually start talking about the meat of the eBook - the problem. This is something you've already introduced in the sales letter itself, but by going through the problem, you're able to introduce the solutions (or strategies, or tips, etc.).

- **The Solution** - This is really the heart of the eBook... The solutions. Fixes. Strategies. Chapters. Content. All that stuff. This is what you brainstormed in an earlier chapter!

- **The Close** - The last section of the eBook is where you close everything out. Normally, an effective way to close an eBook is to include a recap of what someone learned by reading AND also tell them what to do next... Examples are, "visit my website," or "register for the webinar."

NOTE: *One very important tip when talking about eBooks... Make sure you include links in your eBook so a reader can continue their relationship with you through your website. This includes links to landing pages, surveys, blog posts, training material, or whatever else you have in your quiver. eBooks are a very effective method of driving leads and traffic to your site if you use them correctly!*

What You'll Need to Create an eBook

Realistically, all you need to get your eBook done is a word processor like Microsoft Word or Pages for Mac. If you're looking for a processor other than those two common ones, you can also use Google Docs or Open Office, which is the open source Word competitor.

Each of those software tools allows you to export your finished document as a PDF. After you have finished converting the document to a PDF, any reader using any reading platform is going to be able to read it on their computer, tablet, or phone.

Luckily, our smart devices generally do the work for us and allow us to view PDF's through different viewers, like Kindle or iBooks.

A finished word document isn't going to look professional without a cover. If you know a little about Adobe Photoshop, you should be able to use CoverActionPro. A nice looking cover or bundle will be a definite attention grabber for your potential readers and it gives your product a more tangible feel.

If you are walking around in a bookstore, you'll notice beautifully designed covers. Without covers, people wouldn't be able to differentiate the overall feel of the book. Covers convey emotion and grab the reader.

With eBooks, people realize they're purchasing the information, the same as a book. However, you can still give them that feeling as if they're getting a total package, something that they can feel tied to.

You can easily get eBook covers designed at freelance websites like Upwork.com or Fiverr.com pretty cheaply. Both sites are very easy to use. There, you can post a job saying that you need a cover done and give some brief graphical elements as well as a theme to bidders.

After you post your job, you'll get bids from freelancers that would like to work on your job at a price. That way, you're in control as far as what kind of design background you want your freelancer to have.

Once the design is finished, then you have your image file for your PDF.

eBook Formats

There are a few different eBook formats that authors should be familiar with. Truthfully, there is really nothing different between reports, guides, and eBooks in terms of delivery, but sometimes, they're perceived differently to an end user.

- **Report** - A report generally is 8-20 pages, and it's something you give away for free as a lead generation tool or sell for $2 to $9. These shorter PDF documents have value, but typically step through a rather simple process. The simple process is used to bond your readers to you, as we talked about in the previous chapter.

- **Guide** - A guide is typically 20-40 pages or so, and goes more in depth than a report, and is pretty in-depth on one topic. Usually, guides are priced for $17 - $27. 20-40 pages is enough space to walk a customer through a solution, while revealing a simple framework that you can use to create a full blown course (more on this later!)

- **eBook** - eBooks are usually 40 pages to 100+ pages. I've seen them up into 300 pages. It just depends on how much you want to talk about. eBook's are generally sold for $37 to $47 when they're on their own site. On Kindle or iBooks, they're anywhere between $4 and $15 (so it pays to have each of your eBooks on its own sales page!)

These three ebook formats are pretty self-explanatory, but let's take a look at an example.

Within the digital photography niche, a report might contain an incredible strategy on taking portraits of people outside, with guidance on lighting and backgrounds. It has to be enough to draw the reader in to want more information.

Offering a guide in digital photography could include how to take wedding photos of outdoor weddings. You would offer more advice in taking portraits to next level, like capturing emotion within the event itself.

An eBook, the longest format, might include reviews on cameras, accessories you'll need for digital photography, different styles of capturing photos, and important aspects in capturing different emotions and moments within an event.

Dealing With Refunds

For as much as I like eBooks and digital products, there's a caveat that you need to be aware of. There are people who are professional refunders. No matter what they buy, they refund it.

It's in your best interest to offer a guarantee on your product because it increases sales, but there are still a few bad apples in the bunch. For any merchant processor you are using, or for Clickbank; you have to offer a guarantee.

Within the United States, every purchase has a 30 day money back guarantee, whether you state it along with your product or not. The unfortunate situation with a digital product is that the information is just sitting on their hard drive... So whether or not they refund, they keep the product anyway.

How to Price eBooks

The typical price for an eBook is normally $27 to $47 when you sell them on your site with a sales video, with $37 being the most common. The higher end of $47 price point is becoming more popular on some of the information that is published on specialized topics.

There are eBooks out there that are priced $97, $297 and even $397 as well – so consider this as a rough guide! Those topics that carry the higher dollar amounts are usually very specialized though.

Selling eBooks on tablets kills your pricing, though. Price points are quite a bit lower because the marketplace, like the Kindle Marketplace and iBooks sells it for you. With a marketplace, you don't have the ability to develop a true sales message like you can on your own site. However, you're exposed to lots more potential buyers on a marketplace platform.

With a marketplace platform, you have to stick with product prices between $5 and $15 usually. You also have to pay a percentage to the company, the marketplace, as well.

On Amazon for instance, each sale will give either 35% or 70% to the company, depending on how you set up your eBook inside the Marketplace.

Video Course Creation

eBooks are incredible tools and they serve as a great gateway into digital product creation. In certain instances, videos serve a better training medium though.

Videos are becoming a very common form of product creation online, and for a good reason. Bandwidth is readily available to customers, and the internet is easily accessible to most clientele.

Audio and visual learning is a widely used for online learning... With thousands of online universities and knowledge training platforms, video is how education happens. So whether or not you are comfortable on video doesn't matter, it's where technology is headed.

You can get a very nice camera and a tripod and even a green screen and lightning for very little money. In fact, you probably have a way to capture video right now, in your pocket, that will be more than enough when it comes to teaching your students!

Recording yourself isn't very hard, but it can be nerve racking to do full-motion videos so if you feel more comfortable recording just your screen, you can. Simple video capture software like <u>Camtasia</u> or <u>Screenflow</u> will work great for you.

Video courses are great tools for buyers to see, watch, and learn the material. eBooks are nice, but most customers will rather watch a video course. They want to see you, hear you, and learn from you... Video makes it happen.

3 Ways To Teach

There basically three different modalities, or ways to fulfill your education... Text. Audio. Or video. In this day and age, video is the most popular.

Video offers a visual aspect, so you can teach through a presentation, , screen recordings, or by capturing full motion video.

Your students not only hear the words you use, but if you're doing full motion video, with an iPhone or Android device perhaps, they will learn and connect with you through your body language.

If you're doing screen recordings of PowerPoint presentations, you can read through the presentation and offer stories and experiential learning antidotes, similar to how a college professor would teach a class...

One of the biggest benefits to creating video first is that it gives you the ability to 'repurpose' your content...

Say you create a video and want to then convert it to text for an eBook, workbook or some other download. All you would need to do is send it to a transcriptionist or hire someone on the popular Upwork.com outsourcing portal.

There, it can be transcribed into a word document. And, you can export the audio from the video file and turn it into an audio only download.

So by creating the video first, you only have to do things once, and end up delivering multiple formats through your course, adding value or splitting each format out as its own offer.

Types of Video Courses

Your comfort level in front of a camera is going to most likely dictate whether you're going to do full motion videos for our course content or stick to screen recordings.

If you are comfortable presenting the information and capturing yourself on video, then there is very little work that needs to be done leading up to the course creation.

However, many people are not comfortable with the idea of seeing themselves in video. Screen capture software like Camtasia or Screenflow gives you the ability to record your computer screen, capturing your video course without having to stand up and present the material "live."

Using screen capture software, you can easily capture, edit and encode video which can be put together in a membership course for easy access, both on desktop and mobile.

Many of your customers will prefer screen capture videos as course material because it is easy to follow along and is somehow more complete than full motion video. By creating slides before hand and then presenting them, you're able to give a more complete roadmap to a process or strategy. If you're simply capturing yourself on camera, you may leave something out.

Additionally, screen capture videos give you the ability to go right online and show customers whatever you need to, or even walk them through complex processes.

A word of warning... Being comfortable in front of the camera doesn't necessarily make for a good presentation though. When someone is watching you, the words that come out of your mouth only make up a fraction of what's being said by a student... The majority of the information being conveyed is through body language. So, the actual information you're trying so hard to get your students to grasp may not get conveyed correctly unless you are on point with your words AND with your presentation skills.

The Process of Creating a Video Course

Creating a video course is very similar to writing an ebook... Except for the video part of course!

1. The first thing you need to do is brainstorm the topic. Create a training outline or a mind map of all the stuff you want to cover, as discussed in previous chapters.

2. Create PowerPoint slides or write a script for the presentation. PowerPoint seems to be a tad easier, it gives you the ability to use more flowing language than a script, plus you can offer main points through bullets and then give solid backgrounds on those main points.

3. Then, use either a video camera or screen capture software to record (Camtasia or Screenflow) your content. You most likely won't need much if you're doing screen capture. If you're doing traditional, full motion video, an iPhone will work just fine!

4. After you record your video, you'll need to 'encode' it. Basically, that's really fancy terminology for exporting the video into a format that any computer can read. The most popular file formats are *.mov* and *.mp4*. You can alternatively export as *.avi* or *.wmv* as well.

5. Then, it gets a little bit tricky. Because video takes up so much bandwidth, you're not going to want to put it on the same server as your website. Nor, will you want to put it on YouTube because it's public! So, you can:

1. Use a tool called Wistia. Wistia charges a monthly fee but will keep all your videos safe and secure, and provide the ability to play them on your website without slowing anything down! It also makes all your videos iPad and mobile friendly, and has video analytics.

1. Set up an Amazon S3 account and video player plugin on your site. If you're more technical, this will be easy for you. If not, choose Wistia.

6. After your videos are uploaded, copy and paste the embed code on the page of your site that you want your videos to play on!

7. That's it! It might sound like a lot but do it a few times and you'll be golden.

Selling Video Courses

There are a number of ways you can go about selling your videos online, depending on what your goals are.

- You can sell your videos individually by breaking them up into components.

- You can sell them as a group in a 'video training suite,' which is the preferred method, by putting them together into courses or modules.

- You can sell a series of videos delivered weekly through an email auto responder or through a membership site by 'dripping content.' Dripping content means that your customer will get access to certain, set videos every so often. That might be daily, weekly, or monthly. Dripped content is effective for two reasons:

  - Your buyer stays with you longer, meaning your retention is higher.

  - Your buyer doesn't get overloaded with video and course material all at the same time, so they'll be less likely to burn out. This is something you, as the course creator and teacher, will have to manage especially for longer courses.

The Pitfalls of Video Courses

Unfortunately, you'll encounter situations where you get a new user who gets very overwhelmed at how much content there is to go through.

Most course formats are very logical in that they start at a fundamental level, creating a common ground for all students, and then build on top of those fundamentals.

…Some customers will come in and try to do it all at once, and it becomes a very daunting experience for them.

There generally isn't that much information there, but you should give your customers the ability to split it up into smaller pieces or chunks of material, usually called "Modules," with breaks so they can actually applying the training to their lives.

You can still give them access to the entire course, just be aware that this may happen.

The other option is to forcibly break the training up in order to have weekly training modules. Some students, if they pay full price at the outset, will want it all at once… So, if it's done, it's probably best to fulfill for them.

Turning Your Video Courses into DVDs

In an age where technology is everywhere and expanding rapidly, it seems that there is less of a need to offer DVD's, but there are still people out there that want to watch them. It's pretty easy to stream video from a tablet to a television using a Roku or an Apple TV. But, it is still a good option to give buyers a choice.

In niches like health and fitness, DVD's still sell. Creating DVD's out of your videos is easily done using a service like disc.com. Basically you create the video, upload it to the website, and they just mail the disc out for you.

For the technical specs, you'll want to make sure your video is at least 720 pixels wide, with 1080 pixels being preferable. The benefit to also offering a DVD is that you can actually offer it on Amazon FBA and they'll ship it for you!

Video Training Best Practices

Video is considered the standard in digital education right now, but since it's a newer technology (streaming video that was created on a personal computer...), there are a lot of grey areas where video courses are concerned. Not to mention, so many course creators use their course format to convey their personal style and brand.

Although there isn't a 'best practices' guide per se on video courses, we have been selling them in our business and for our clients for a LONG time now, so we have seen quite a bit of feedback.

The following are some guidelines for your video course:

- **Course length** - Usually, video courses tend to be 5 to 7 modules or sections long. From there, there are usually 4-6 videos in each module.

- **Video length** – You want your students to watch your videos (of course!). The best length to encourage consumption is 5 to 7 minutes long, with each video centering around one topic. If the video is more tutorial based, like walking someone through a piece of software or a more complicated procedure, then up to 20 minutes is fine.

- **Video Transcripts** - Customers love to be able to print out the PowerPoint, notes, or transcripts of the video to read and take notes on.

How to Price Your Video Course

One thing that's never set in stone with video courses is a price. Sometimes you'll come across a free video course that is based on some really great information, and sometimes you'll see $3,000 courses that have added in some components like live training calls and coaching.

The price of your video course depends on the content and the perceived value that it has built up to within the sales message. If you are teaching somebody how to become a millionaire, then the video course itself can be more expensive because the perceived value and eventual payoff is higher.

If you're teaching somebody how to crochet, it's going to be a cheaper video course because it's not an investment that yields monetary results… It's just something that your students wish to learn.

Typically, video courses start out between $67 and $97. That's a decent starting spot for the first product that somebody sees from you.

More expensive and informative products follow suit, either as an upsell sequence or sold over the phone. If your course is very selective and specialized, there is room for it to be priced higher because of the specialized scope of the information you teach on.

For example, if you have a general business marketing course, your price might be $97. If your course is targeted specifically towards service-based professionals, it can be $397 or $497 because of customization and focus.

As a guideline, anything above $1,000 typically has some live elements included, like webinars, group coaching calls, and more personalized attention.

Closing Thoughts on Creating Video Courses

To close out the video section, I want to leave you with some thoughts and notes that we've learned through years of offering them.

Make sure your videos are as secure as possible and not available to the public.

You don't want your videos out there for anyone in the world to watch without paying. Wistia.com is a great resource that lets you protect your content and stream it to any web page that you wish. Don't trust your revenue producing course content and videos with public services like YouTube.

Your audio levels should be constant in all of your packaged videos.

I generally use one microphone through an entire recording session. I don't move it, unplug it, or mess with settings. I also try to make sure it's adjusted the same way every time. I would encourage you very much to do the same. Other product creators have computers that are designated for recording audio and video and that's all they're used for.

Tools for capturing video

Easily enough, iPhones and Android mobile devices capture video just as well as any camera out there.

To capture your computer screen, you're going to need either Camtasia or Screenflow on a Mac. Jing is a free software tool also available but has quite a few limitations in terms of the length of videos you can record and editing capabilities.

As for webcams and mics, most laptops anymore have a great webcam attached to them, especially on a Mac.

For microphones, I use podcasting setups or good headphones. Basically, any headset with a mic will work. If you're looking for a standalone mic, there's the Blue Yeti and the Audiotechnica A2020. The A2020 is the one I use for everything.

Audio Course Creation

Audio products are quite a bit less complicated after going through what it takes to create a video product... There is a bit less setup, but you do lose the important visual component of learning your customers may appreciate.

Audio does have its benefits though:

- You don't necessarily have to script the PowerPoint, so they're really quick and easy to create.

- Audio products lend themselves to portability, so your customers can load them on your mp3 players, mobile devices, or listen to them on their computers.

- Audio can also be transcribed into e-books and books, which is a very popular way of 'writing' books now. Authors record themselves and give the content to a transcriptionist.

- And, at the end of the day, audio courses are pretty much the simplest type of product to create.

A few years ago, I was out of town at a conference. One night, while in the hotel, I had an idea for a course... Everyone was in their hotel rooms, being wiped from being in the room, so I decided to Mindmap it out and start recording.

In only three hours that one night, I recorded an info product that I spent the next 3 years selling, making well into six-figures...

I sent the .mp3 files to a transcriptionist, who emailed me back a 90 page book and I started selling it online.

Audio gives you the ability to do many different things... It's easy to listen to. It's portable and easily accessible. You can have your customers listening to it while they're skiing, mowing the lawn, or doing the dishes.

Typically, I don't start with audio courses. I create the video course itself and then pull the audio our of it, creating an .mp3 file. That way, the hard work (creating the course), and I can offer the total package together all bundled and ready to go.

You don't have to do it that way.

The first product customers might see offered from you might be an eBook. Then from there, potentially an audio course, which leads to a video course.

While it might all be the same content, people will appreciate that they can buy different versions of the product to suit their needs.

Creating an Audio Product

The process of creating an audio product is fairly simple.

1. You brainstorm your product the same way you do a video course or an eBook, by mindmapping it. You start with your central idea in the middle, and then add layers to it.

2. Plug your headphones or mic into your computer.

3. Open up a freely available program called Audacity. Do a Google search for it. You'll also need a plugin to export it to an .mp3 file available here.

4. Install and open up Audacity.

5. Hit record!

6. Once you're done, you can edit the audio if you like, cutting out any verbal imperfections. You don't have to though - it's up to you. Listeners like it when you're authentic.

7. Then, export the file in .mp3 format!

That's it! You've got your .mp3 files for your audio product!

As long as you have a good mindmap our outline of your course, you can get right into recording it. If you're the kind of person that needs to script it out a little more, then you should begin with taking more detailed notes, so you don't forget major points.

If your topic material is something you are an expert in, you'll most likely be able to talk through it with minimal hesitation.

Creating an Audio Product by Interviewing Others

Another way of creating an audio project is by interviewing experts in the field. This gives you "credibility by association" as well as actual information that you'll be selling. You can then use their expertise to build your own brand. We will get more in depth on leveraging experts in our next chapter on tele-seminars... In terms of technology, teleconferencing software, like Skype, is the easiest way to interview an expert.

Creating Audio Products with Teleconference Software

The idea behind a teleconference is that you are able to meet with multiple people over the phone, in real time. There can be three people on the line all talking or there might be 500 people dialed in listening to one person, depending on what you are trying to do.

Most teleconferencing companies allow you to record the call, which makes it easy to use for interviewing purposes. Not to mention, these companies have been around for decades and there are many that offer these services... Two tried-and-trusted companies are GoToWebinar.com and and UberConference.com.

GoToWebinar.com is webinar and virtual meeting software, but you can only use the audio functionality and run teleconferences for up to 1000 people. You get all the functionality you could want including sharing video, sharing cameras, recording, asking questions, surveys, etc.

Uberconference.com is what I use for conference calling with my clients. It's like a normal bridge line, but there isn't a call-in number. You can share video with a Google Chrome extension, record and a lot more.

Creating Interview-Style Audio Products

Selling a a collection of interviews is a fairly common way of creating an audio product. For example, if your niche is digital photography, you might interview:

- A portrait photography expert

- A nature or landscape photographer

- A lighting expert

- A popular wedding photographer

- And the editor at a photography magazine

Now, package those interviews together and you have a digital audio product!

You can also send those audio files to a transcriptionist and create eBooks out of them. 60 minutes' worth of audio will usually give you anywhere between 30 and 60 pages of text, so it's pretty easy to get an eBook out of an interview.

Thoughts on Audio Products

By now, you should be able to understand the endless possibilities surrounding audio products. On the market, there are:

- Audio books

- Interviews

- Teleseminar series

- Radio shows with guests

- Podcasts

If the content you are organizing and collecting has value, you can sell it individually or offer access to the whole collection...

You can either bundle audio sessions together, or sell them individually. You can even sell tele-seminars and interviews, or use them as a starting point to promote your brand.

Audio content is usually priced a little higher than eBooks and reports, but not as high as video, for obvious reasons.

Usually, audio products sell for around $37-$67. If you're bundling audio files together or your material is highly specialized, pricing could be as high as $297. If you're shipping the audio files to your customers on CD, you can even get away with product prices up to $997.

Also, if you're including transcripts with the purchase, it's important to know that they don't have to be perfect. They'll read like transcripts, but as long as you get someone to omit all of your natural speaking mistakes, like "oh" and "um," they'll be fine.

What You'll Need for Audio Products

Here's what you're going to need to create audio products:

- A podcasting microphone or headphones with audio input.

- Audacity, which is software for recording audio on your computer. You can use fancier stuff, but Audacity is all you really need.

- (Optional) Conferencing software like GoToMeeting/GoToWebinar, Uberconference or Skype.

To sell these audio products, the files will need to be downloadable, which means that they'll need to be in .mp3 format. Your buyers will then be able to import the file directly into their media player or phone.

Tele-seminars & Summits

In this chapter, we're going to talk about one of the first types of digital products I had experience with when my business began; tele-seminars and summits.

Tele-seminars are one of the easiest ways to grow your email list and produce next to immediate revenue in your business.

A tele-seminar is a lot like a webinar, just without the video. So essentially, you put together a Tele-seminar Series on something in your market... Then you invite people to it!

Not to mention, tele-seminars are brilliant money makers if you aren't an expert, of if you don't already have an audience...

To start, you organize experts around a specific topic and schedule a to interview them. You should begin by searching Google and Amazon.com for authors, bloggers, speakers and industry leaders. Then, email or call them, seeing if they're open to being interviewed on your tele-seminar series.

The tele-seminar series works because you are allowing experts to capitalize on their experience. Not only will your tele-seminar gain exposure and grow their own brand, but these experts may sell more copies of their work as well!

If each of these experts has a list of 5,000 or 10,000 people, you can ask them to let their list know about their appearance on your tele-seminar series, helping you grow your audience VERY quickly!

One of the qualifiers that I've used in the past when finding experts to be interviewed is simply asking them how many people they have on their email list. If it's over 5,000 people – you're good. If they don't have a list or they have less than 5,000 people – move on. The goal for you, besides sharing great content and generating revenue, is to build your brand in the space.

Now, in addition to the email list, you should also make sure that your experts are offering something for sale on their call. When they make a sale, you get a commission. The commission is whatever you negotiate, but it's usually 50%.

The pitch can be simple, too...

> "Hey, if you liked this call and want more expert tips and tricks, I've got a course for you. For only $67 you'll get 12 videos, downloadable reports, etc... Just go to http://domainname.com/ to get started.

So, as a tele-seminar series organizer:

- You'll make money selling the downloads of the recordings (and the transcripts) following the series.

- You'll grow your email list, piggybacking off of the experts in the industry

- You'll make a commission on everything the experts are selling

- You'll be seen as expert yourself, leveraging other people's authority and credibility in the industry!

The hardest person to get to agree to a tele-seminar series is always the first person... After you get the commitment from the first expert, you should be talking about it to the next person you ask to join you...

The process then turns into a waterfall, hopefully with you gaining more experienced guests in the meantime. As the list gets longer and more prestigious, those more renowned experts will have a lot harder of a time saying no.

Notes on Teleseminar Series

Here are some general notes on running a profitable tele-seminar series that you can use to grow your brand online...

Charge for downloads.

As you create and offer downloads, make sure you are charging for them.

Simple downloads are a great way to generate revenue. Don't give free replays either. Many customers in the market will just assume that because they signed up for the event that they are going to be able to review it whenever they want.

Make sure that's not the case, because your content is valuable.

At the very most, give your customers access to a replay for up to 24 hours. After that, you shouldn't be giving away free material.

Get commissions from your interviewees/experts.

The perks of having experts on your tele-seminar is that both of you can make some cash.

Make sure you make an affiliate commission on anything sold on the calls themselves. If your expert speaker is selling something, make sure you make a cut, usually around 50%.

Also, make sure you give away affiliate commission on any downloads sold.

Overall

Tele-seminar series can make you an incredible amount of money. I have had clients do $17,000 and generate 14,000 subscriber email lists in three weeks with no list and no presence in a market.

When I first started online, I met a guy in the 'raw foods' market who organized a tele-seminar series as his first foray into that market... He made over $100,000 and built a 40,000 person list in under a month. After you build up your list, you can live on it for years to come.

What you'll need to run a Tele-seminar Series

Here's what you're going to need to start a tele-seminar series:

- A way to process payments – Ontraport.com, Stripe.com, Paypal.com, Clickbank.com, Samcart.com...

- Affiliate software – Ontraport.com, Samcart.com, iDevAffiliate.com, Infusionsoft.com, Clickbank.com

- Access to a conference call line – GoToMeeting/ GoToWebinar.com, Uberconference.com

Overall, tele-seminars generate money and email lists more quickly and efficiently than other ways, without the headaches and finding customers to mail.

They are, however, a hassle to set up because you have to organize all of the interviewees!

Workbooks

Workbooks can be used to add value to your digital product, usually bundled with other digital files. When you sell an eBook, video, or audio course, it could be worthwhile to sell a workbook as a bonus or an add-on to your digital product.

The point of a workbook is for the customer to have something to solidify the material and training that you're putting them through – to tie to the product and the experience.

Presenting tutorials and graphics for expanded learning throughout the course can be a great way to further educate your audience.

If you aren't graphically inclined, the best way to create a workbook for your course is:

- Draw the pages out on paper, including where you want your students to take notes and diagrams for expanded learning.

- Post the project on Upwork.com, looking for a graphic designer do it for you.

- Look through the bidders portfolios and see if they've completed something similar to what you're looking for…

- Award the project!

After the workbook is designed, you can either print it out and ship it to your customer or offer it as a PDF below each training module.

Taking it a step further, you can even have your students assemble the material so that they can reference back to it after the course is over, such as putting each packet into a three ring binder.

The workbook can either be priced into the course, adding value… Or, you can give it away as a free bonus for all students who sign up! In a lot of cases, having an interactive element like a workbook REALLY ups the value of the course, meaning you can charge a lot more.

Memberships

Membership courses integrate both the the course material material and technology for prospects who want to learn more about any subject. One of the reasons why membership courses are highly used is because they're pretty easy to set up and they lock non-buyers out of the course material so only your customers get access.

… And to put it simply, membership courses are the most lucrative form of digital products because there is a recurring, subscription payment. This form of product allows you to sell a member just once and they continue to pay until they cancel their membership.

Now, memberships take on all shapes and sizes… A customer may buy a membership for course material, or the Facebook group, or the forum, or access to the expert… But typically, there is a foundational sort of content to a membership made up of course material… In other words, Training made up of in the form of text and video. Sometimes, the membership material also includes audio.

The courses that I've sold in the past and most of my client projects have all incorporated educational content, typically video. Using that video, it's relatively easy to extract the audio and have a transcriptionist turn the material into a text file or ebook – so video serves as the anchor to each of the educational formats.

When I originally looked at starting a membership site way back in the day, people were charging as much as $5,000 to simply set up a membership. Now, it's a lot higher. If you are willing to put in some work and learn about access levels, member privileges and the like; you can set one up for about $200 and run it all yourself.

The easiest way to set up a membership site is to build one using WordPress. You can design the site any way you want and name it whatever you like. Finding a template that fits your business and brand is pretty easy since WordPress is so widely adopted...

The most important piece to a membership site is the plug-in that powers all of the membership functionality. The one we use is called WishList Member. WishList integrates easily with WordPress, and can lock down all your course material page by page. That way, if a non-member visits the site and tries to view the content, they'll be directed to either a membership login screen or your sales material.

WishList Member has a very complete set of training videos to follow when you first get started, as well as a "Quick Setup" option that'll create the pages you need for your membership site. You can further customize the payment gateway, email autoresponder settings, shopping cart, affiliate tools and lots more.

Once you set up the integrations inside the plugin, it's time to start adding content and setting up membership privileges accordingly. If you have a couple of different levels of membership, make sure that only specified content is available for certain levels. Don't allow non-members too much access, but enough to draw them in to purchase a membership. You can even give them a sneak peek into the material, like the first 100 words of a blog post, as a preview. Then, they can make the choice to purchase or not.

With the content you're making available to your members, you want to be sure you use what's known as a "drip feed" system. Inside WishList, it's set up under the "Sequential Upgrade" tab. When you offer all of the content inside your membership, it's more than likely that your members will be overwhelmed.

…If you offer drip content, you'll be able to send out a bit of information that encourages people through the course, module by module.

One thing is for sure though, you always want to keep your customers excited about the content, especially around the monthly billing period. If you can tease new training or a new update right around when someone's monthly membership renews, they'll stick with you for longer.

Another way to generate some revenue inside a membership is to make use of affiliate offers… Affiliate offers should be placed in the sidebar and alongside your content, inside your membership. When a member accesses your course, it's likely that something will catch their eye and they'll click through on the offer.

If the affiliate offers are well placed and interesting, you might end up generating extra revenue just off of those affiliate purchases. So, not only are you making money from your subscription, you're also making money because members are purchasing affiliate products.

Another thing you can do to incentivize affiliate purchases is by giving away bonuses. If you can give a bonus that is cohesive with the membership site and the training, it's a perfect way to organize a promotion around a secondary course or offer. That can also keep the member payments coming because your members feel rewarded!

Forums, Facebook Group access and live training calls are additional ways of adding value to your membership and creating community. They foster a group mentality in your membership, where your subscribers can be self-supportive, asking questions and offering advice.

And last by not least, always keep in touch with your members. Use surveys to find out what they want to do next. You can get on a group coaching call with some of your members and throw around a lot of good content, but always ask what they want next...

Let them know they have a voice. If they need more training in a certain area, you can provide it for them to keep subscription payments rolling in. If you're unable to provide expertise on the subject, find someone who can. You can always approach an expert in the field and tell them about your site, what the training needs are, and what you're willing to pay them for a few hours worth of content. Then, you can pass on the training to your members.

Associations

Similar to membership sites, associations foster community and live off of subscription revenue. The basics of the "Association Model" are community, content and passion. You want to pull together a group of people all sharing similar interests in something they're deeply passionate about, and offer training or content aligned with that passion.

Some things that an association publishes are trainings, forums, social profiles, and industry news. There are probably tons of local associations around you right now. Think about local gun clubs, snowmobiling clubs, Chambers of Commerce, business networking forums, etc. Those are all examples of associations that you pay to be a member of. Sometimes the cost is $10 per month, sometimes its $400 per year; but you don't need to be local to put members in an association.

Associations have many different names. They can be referred to as:

- Syndicates

- Forums
- Alliances
- Memberships
- Collectives

Pricing for these associations should be almost negligible and encourage the stick rate (how long a member continues to pay). Common pricing, depending on the target audience, is $5 to $40 a month.

(With membership sites, stick rate is normally three or four months, meaning a member will stick with you for three or four months, and then leave. You'll have the occasional member stay for longer or shorter than that stick rate, but typically the lifetime of the member falls in that timeframe.)

An association usually needs to be cheap – almost negligible – so members don't bail as often as they would a higher priced subscription. Some of the most successful associations are $5 or $10 a month... The reason being, if you have a $5 charge on your credit card, it's so little that it tends to be more work to call and cancel the membership!

The best example of this is Consumer Reports. The Consumer Reports website has about 1.8 million paying members at $3.95 per month. Their stick rate is years long, because the $3.95 charge to most people is pretty inconsequential. Consumer Reports has amassed millions of users, so it has absolutely jaw-dropping revenue even though it costs less than four dollars per month.

The goal is to encourage interaction between your members so they stay longer and send their friends... You're obviously not going to make too much money by selling 100 members of an association for five dollars a month, but when you get to 10,000 or 50,000 strong, it's a much bigger deal.

10,000 memberships at $9 per month is $90,000 a month in revenue... And since it's less than $10, your churn rate will be exceptionally low! (Churn rate is how many members leave on a monthly basis.)

Now, the most successful associations are formed around a common cause. You can have that association be business related, or focused on a hobby; like guns, snowmobiles, fishing, photography, crafts, quilting, and so on and so forth. The trick is to find the common ground with your members and then build for them.

I have a friend who has a gun club and he receives about $450,000 a month in membership does. Those members never leave, because they have a common ground and a common enemy (aka the government) that they play up every chance they get.

Encouraging interaction between your members can be done in a forum or a Facebook Group, giving members a chance to be seen and be heard. Some of those association members may just be great candidates to moderate the group or answer particularly pressing questions. If you get one or two members that post a lot and gain a following of sorts, you can give them more responsibility in the group.

PART THREE: TOOLS & TECH

Tools & Software

Now that we have the fundamentals of brainstorming, creating and packaging course content; it's time to execute... To put it all together.

This, my friend, is where the rubber meets the road. I will warn you though, it's very easy to get a little overwhelmed, especially if you're new to websites and digital marketing, so take it easy.

In this chapter, we'll talk about the tools you'll need to have a great website set up, with product sales. There is some groundwork that needs to be covered before we're ready to go though...

We need to make sure that:

- Your customer's payments will be processed

- Your email marketing is in place along

- Your website is built and focused on SELLING

If things aren't set up correctly from the start, you'll end up hitting some roadblocks that'll derail your momentum... It's ok though - all of this stuff is easy to set up and get running - you just need the right tools.

To start your website, at the very least you're going to need a domain name and web hosting.   The easiest place to do both is at Hostgator.com… It's economical hosting that's pretty reliable.

Once you choose a domain name and go through the process or ordering it, Hostgator will email you the access to the control panel. From the control panel, you want to install WordPress, which is the content management system that powers all of our websites.

Now, the easy part…   Once WordPress is installed, there are lots of things you **can** do. WordPress grew up as blogging software and has really become a fully featured content management system.   It can be a little rough to get started with though if technology isn't your thing.

I created a secondary piece of software that builds all of your marketing pages and puts them on your site… It's called the Scriptly Page Builder. You can learn more about it here:

http://scriptly.org/builder/

Scriptly Members can create landing pages, webinar registration pages, sales pages, confirmation pages and lots more…   And then they can add them to their WordPress site through a plugin so they get all of the marketing functionality to convert visitors to buyers… And none of the complicated setup that you usually go through!

If you're going to manage a membership so your customers have to log in to get access to your content, there is not plugin better than Wishlist Member. It integrates with all the popular shopping carts and allows you to offer a section of your website that is only accessible to your customers.

To make a long story short, Wishlist Member is a membership plugin that sits inside your WordPress website and uses the WordPress infrastructure. You can log into your Admin Dashboard and manage your members, access, control which pages are accessible to members or general public, and more. Wish List also has some useful training videos.

After you get your website up and running, you'll want to be able to collect leads and build email lists of your prospects, buyers, and affiliates. There are LOTS of options on the market that serve as an email marketing CRM... Too many to list. All of them have advantages and disadvantages with the more expensive tools very difficult to use... And the cheaper tools majorly lacking in functionality.

Convertly is another tool that we've built, specifically for helping business owners automate their marketing in an easy, streamlined way.

To check out Convertly, go to:

http://convertly.org

Once you set up your email marketing software, you'll want to make sure to add a few different types of lists... All in all, you'll have three different lists for your product.

You'll have:

- A prospect list for those who haven't purchased yet

- A buyers list for those that have...

- And an affiliate list for your Joint Venture partners or affiliates who help you promote.

Each of those lists will should be treated differently, always having the next thing you want them to do in mind.

- Your prospect list will receive promotions specific to buying the product plus any affiliate products you want to promote.

- The buyers list is for fulfilling the product, bonding to your customers, and promoting affiliate products after they've had a chance to consume the thing they bought from you

- Your affiliate list is used to keep all of your affiliates in the loop about latest and greatest with your product.

Once you have your website set up, you'll need a shopping cart finalized so people can purchase your products and you get paid...

Again, there are plenty of options...

- Samcart

- Paypal

- Clickbank

- Ontraport

In terms of simple shopping carts, Samcart is about the best there is. Their shopping cart pages convert hands down better than any other out of the box solution. They integrated with lots of payment processors. And, they're easy to set up.

If you're looking for a simple way to get money, albeit not the best for conversion, it's Paypal. You can set up a Paypal button simply enough so you can get paid for your stuff…

ClickBank is the third option. ClickBank will allow you to set up a shopping cart for one product or in a sequence of upsells and downsells. The fantastic thing about ClickBank is that it not only allows you to sell your products, but it has a community of affiliates that will promote your products for you. It works as a shopping cart as well as an affiliate management application with its own network of affiliates.

Ontraport (and Infusionsoft) both are big-gun software tools that really work to combine a lot of your digital business solutions. Ontraport is an all in one business and marketing platform designed for information marketers, experts, and coaches. They do the normal email marketing, but they also do physical postcards through the mail, different types of shopping cart functionality, and a lot of affiliate tracking. They also have a WordPress integration, so you can set up membership sites and then have it all work through the same platform. Pricing is high for a startup but it's a complete solution if your business is ready for it.

In terms of additional tools that you may find helpful…

- **Curately** is a blog content curation software, helping you put together high quality content for your website and blog easily. Learn more at **http://curately.org/**

- **Askly** is a survey and quiz tool for engaging with your visitors and figuring out what they want more of. The software app features quizzes and surveys that convert more of your respondents giving you more actionable intel on them. Visit http://askly.org/ to sign up for free.

- **TimeSlots** is an online schedule tool. Give your visitors a link and they can book a time on your calendar and answer any questions you might have for them. It's perfect for coaches, consultants and sales people who are selling a high ticket service. Sign up for free at http://timeslots.org/.

- **Statly** is an analytics and stats solution for tracking website visitors from the moment they first hit your website, all the way until when they purchase and after. It's designed to show you where you sales are coming from and what marketing channel is responsible for sending them. You can sign up for free at **http://statly.org/.**

- **Zendesk** is a support desk, so that your users, members, and buyers can email support requests in and you can track whether or not the question was answered, how quick and efficient the process was, along with other data.

- **FreshBooks** is also a great invoicing program if you're a coach or consultant... They tie in with LOTS of bookkeeping services and other things that'll help you get paid.

- **MindMeister** is a great tool for mindmapping. You can pull up MindMeister on your browser, phone, iPad, or whatever device you're using and just get started. That way, if you have an idea throughout your process and you're on the go, you can just pull out your phone and add whatever you need to.

- **BaseCamp** is project management from a web worker sense. Once your products take off, you can utilize BaseCamp to assign actions for projects to multiple team members where they have the ability to work on the project or leave notes for others to check out and incorporate. BaseCamp is great for keeping people on task should you have a larger project to work on with a lot of clients.

- **Upwork** is a great place to find freelance workers for your projects. You can post a project, define the terms of the project, and then have the freelancers submit the bid for the job. The bids allow you to go through each freelancer, see their experience with similar jobs, the feedback they've received, and the amount they can do the job for. You can then make an informed decision about who you'd like to hire for a particular project.

- **Facebook** can easily be used for networking. A lot of higher level people use Facebook to communicate and keep in touch with friends, family and associates. It's a little less stressful to find someone on Facebook and message than it is to find their email online

- **LinkedIn** is a professional social networking site. The contacts you find on Linkedin tend to be a little more high profile, as are the relationships that you form there. Being that it's business-centric, you have usually find a lot more information out about the professionally... Making Linkedin's search bar a must-use tool!

- **Skype** is used as a communication tool, and we've already talked about using it for teleconferences. For me, Skype is the primary communication tool especially overseas. Having a Skype ID will get you a lot of face to face time with clients and professionals in your industry, and it puts a face to a name.

Product Creation Tools

The tools you need to get your product created will depend on what type of product you intend to release. You'll definitely need a word processor, so either Microsoft Word or Pages for Mac. You can also use Google Drive which has a free, mobile ready, word processor. At the end of the day, you'll want to have the ability to save or export to document into a PDF format – which all three software platforms support.

If you're planning on creating an audio file, then Audacity at Audacity.SourceForge.com is free and very useful. Install the program, open it up, and start speaking into the computer or laptop's microphone or into the external microphone/headset you have connected.

For capturing video, Camtasia and Screenflow are really useful. Camtasia has versions for both a Windows desktop and for Mac. I personally prefer Screenflow for Mac though... They don't have a Windows version, unfortunately.

Camtasia and Screenflow both capture your computer screen, your webcam and your microphone. Then, you can edit the file and export it into a format that all computers can play, usually an .mp4 file. They're what we use to capture PowerPoint and voice for our courses.

Another benefit to using either Camtasia or Screenflow… They make video editing easy. There is no real need for a complicated video editing tools if you have one of those two applications.

If I capture a webcam video or video through my camera or phone, I can import it into Camtasia and then use all the video editing tools that come with it.

As far as cameras go, you can buy a really high-end camera, but you can realistically produce what you need to with a mobile phone. At the end of the day, a lot of the video quality, especially at the 4K level, is going to be encoded out to make the file sizes more manageable so they stream to your customers computers better.

If you're going to be doing a lot of video camera work, definitely invest in a good wireless lavalier microphone (or wireless lapel mic). You can set up your camera or mobile phone on a tripod and then move without being attached to a long microphone. Not to mention, a good mic will filter out the background noise so your videos are a little more polished!

Setup Notes

So we've spent quite a bit of time going through the types of digital products that you can create and what goes in each of them. The simplest to create are audio and eBooks, and they are the widely accepted. With the various tablet manufacturers pushing digital reading devices, consuming digital content is now mainstream.

Videos give help you educate, nurture, and bond with your prospect in a way that's unparalleled in distance education. Video training has a higher perceived value and you can package or bundle the material in lots of different ways. You can offer video content, locked behind a member's login for your customers to download and stream. You can also export the audio out of those videos, have them transcribed, and include all three formats in your course. Not to mention, video has a very high-perceived value and will fetch you a lot more money!

Audio-only content, such as shipped CD's or an instructional audio .mp3 file that you send in the mail also has high perceived value in the market. Video is the mainstream method of course creation now-a-days though. Of all the formats you can choose to deliver your content, audio, is also easier to create than an eBooks or video. All you need is a mic and a computer, a good Mindmap to work from, and a quiet room to record.

Tele-seminars have an extremely high value, and can generate incredible demand and revenue depending on how you structure it. They also work really well because you're able to leverage other people's audience and experience into your own brand. You don't need to be an expert to do well with the tele-seminar model. What you do need to do is find experts to interview! That's the thing that could be a little time consuming.

Adding a workbook to your course (or giving it away as a bonus of freebie) adds incredible value to your course. Depending on the material of the workbook too, you could also sell it. Typically though, a workbook is going to be a companion offer for your paid material though!

Membership courses are my favorite form of digital product. You can do so much with them, and they have multiple revenue generation methods. Not only can you sell your membership by itself... It gives you monthly revenue or a baked-in higher end offer (the annual commitment!). Plus, you can promote affiliate products or offer higher priced coaching services through the membership as well.

Lastly, associations are great ways to promote longevity and value to a community. Low-priced associations garner more members because cost can be inconsequential to members if they have access to something they may want in the future. Pricing between $5-9 per month is preferred. If you want to charge more, around $27 or $37, you'll need to provide a monthly published report. With a lower price, your stick rate will be much longer than the normal three or four months.

Now, in the next chapter, we'll start to dig into creating your website and your sales material. Now that we have a product to sell (or at least a plan on what we're going to offer!) we need to start putting the front-end pieces in place to sell it!

PART FOUR: THE SETUP

Setting Up Your Online Presence

In order to successfully sell a digital product (or anything for that matter) online, you'll need to understand what a website does, how it's sequenced, and the different elements of a successful sales funnel. This part is going to get pretty deep, so be sure to take your time as you go through it.

In "Convert," the second book in this series, we'll go into much more depth on converting traffic to sales, including specific types of sales funnels that work and where you should apply them. For now though, we're going to detail the areas of the website that should get the most attention, and what needs to be included in each!

In order to sell from a website, you need content and sales copy... That's a given. But there are also a few special pages that you need to put in place – pages that'll handle the heavy lifting when it comes to sales.

Those specialized pages are:

- **A squeeze page or landing page** that collects the email addresses of people who want to receive more information from you. The landing is the first place that we ask for anything from a prospect – in this case it's their permission to contact them through email in the future.

- **A sales page** will act as your "always on" salesman. No matter what time of day or night someone visits your page, they can learn about your product and ultimately buy.

- **A confirmation page** either delivers the product (like an eBook) or tells your new customer what to do next (check their email for their course login. If you're selling a membership, the confirmation page can double as registration page for access to the course.

Some of the setup is going to depend on what format your digital product is in. If it is a video, you're going to want to lock it behind a membership login. If it's an eBook, you'll still probably want make people sign in for it to discourage sharing, but you can send it through email just as effectively.

The next few chapters will cover all of these critical pages in greater details, including what should be where.

In essence, your website is going to be a minimum of two pages, a sales page and a landing page... And a maximum of LOTS of pages, depending on the level of complexity that you want.

If you're planning on putting up a blog, a contact page, a support page, multiple products; then it gets more complicated. At the very minimum though, you need a page selling your product and a page that fulfills the product for your customers...

Now, the content that's on these pages is incredibly important. A simple product description and a buy button probably won't do much to convert your website visitors into sales...

That's why we created Scriptly – to ease the burden of writing sales copy and email copy for product owners.

You can check it out at http://scriptly.org/.

Scriptly writes:

- Email promotion sequences

- Sales videos (or Video Sales Letters if you're familiar with industry jargon!)

- Sales Webinars

Scriptly also builds your landing pages, sales pages, confirmation pages and much, much more...

Sales copywriting is totally different than what you learned in College Writing 101 and you need become intimately aware sales and buyer psychology to pull it off successfully.

Because it's such a crucial element of selling online and it's a skillset that is only ever learned through intense practice, sales copy is going to be the most component when it comes to your website... Unless you're using Scriptly, of course.

Some copywriters charge up to $10,000 just to write the sales copy!

Now, let's dive into the individual pages, what needs to be on them, how they should be structured, and so on!

Your Landing Page

The primary purpose of a squeeze page is to collect a prospective customer's name and email address in exchange for **something.** You want to add them to your email list so you can communicate with them in the future.

Even if these prospects don't buy your product at first, they'll be on your email list and they may buy down the line at some point. If you email them with interesting content and keep your product and brand at the forefront of their mind, you will likely get a sale out of them at some point.

Now, landing pages are structured very specifically...

The Headline

To get started, you will need to have a headline that'll grab your prospects attention immediately as helping them solve a problem that they're currently experiencing in their life.

Examples include:

- Free video reveals _____!

- Discover How To _____ in _____ Days Or Less!

- Learn The Step By Step Process For _____ Without _____

You would be surprised at how often a headline alone can drive people onto your email list. Even small changes, like changing a period at the end of a sentence to an exclamation mark can give you significant improvement!

Quite simply, the headline is to be the most essential part in capturing signups.

Bullets

Bullet points are a HUGE part of your landing page copy. They quickly tell someone exactly what they can expect from you, through shorty, snappy, one line sentences.

The bullet must contact both a feature of the product/service/freebie/ thing AND the benefit that they'll received because of that feature!

Please pay very special attention to that. The bullets must tell your visitors what will happen as a result of downloading your report or signing up for your video

Make sure they're easily understandable.

As an example, here are some bullet points taken right off of our best performing landing page:

Download this FREE report now to...

- Discover the absolute, #1 subject line that you can use for both clicks and opens! (hint: it has a smily face!)

- Find out which "Oops!" email we sent (after we botched an affiliate link) that doubled our sales...

- Learn how to effectively 'pre-frame' a piece of content or blog post, getting the highest clickthrough possible and pre-qualifying our target audience...

- Discover what highest clicked-thru subject line was... (and it wasn't the one with the highest open rate!)

- Plus, a LOT more!

Multimedia content

Another thing you need on your landing page is some form of multimedia content...

That can be:

- A video telling your prospects what they'll receive from you, in exchange for their email address.

- An image of an eCover graphic depicting the download that they're about to receive.

- A screenshot that gives them a peak at what they'll be getting, like a blurry Mindmap or worksheet graphic...

I usually start simply and just get an e-cover graphic done of the report or 'thing' that I'm giving away... Then, that e-cover graphic sits on the landing page as a visual representation of what they're entering their email address to download...

And that leads me to the most important part of a landing page, the lead magnet.

Lead Magnet

Your lead magnet is the thing that your prospects will be downloading. Examples include:

- A report

- An eBook

- Audio .mp3 file

- A free video

- A series of free videos (sometimes called a mini-class)

- A spreadsheet

- A workbook...

The easiest way to figure out what you want to offer in return for signups, is to ask yourself what you get asked for most from your prospects. What content or knowledge is in high demand from your clients or the people you talk to on a daily basis?

Is it someone looking to manage their finances better?

Or someone looking to manage their time more efficiently?

Maybe it's someone who is looking for a way to plan and stick to goals?

What is it that you get asked about most when you speak to your prospects or customers?

Your answer to that question is going to be the content for your lead magnet. Make sure that the stuff you give away, the stuff inside your lead magnet, is very high value content. You want to give away something that's truly going to excite and inspire them to take action. You want them going through your lead magnet thinking, "Wow, I can't believe that he/she is giving all this away for free!"

Believe me – impress them with the lead magnet and they'll be back to buy your digital product before you know it!

Now, let's look at some examples of landing pages... These are all available to you inside Scriptly, this very minute!

This one is the absolute BEST one we've ever tested in terms of conversion rate:

We've spent over $100,000 this year alone in testing out this page and what you see on this page is the winning variation of over 22 split tests.

Is it exceptionally pretty? No. Does it get the point across as to what a prospect is downloading? Absolutely.

This template converts almost as well as the one you just looked at... It's a little prettier but the structure is largely the same...

All of the information goes to a service called Aweber. Aweber allows you do to email marketing right through the platform. Aweber just collects a prospect's email address and name, and then you can compile a list from there.

You'll notice the 'bullets' are arranged as headlines/sub headlines in the dark bar on the page... The 'download' button is also a little more modern.

Then, as a third example, we have a page that doesn't have any multi-media content on it... No image or video. It's a simple page and converts very well for a multi-video series that prospects get access to when they enter their email address..

At the end of the day, the thing you want to emphasize on your landing page that you have a solution to a problem that their facing.

At the end of the day, that's what will get people converted...

Sales Page

Your sales page is the heart of conversion for your course... Your sales page should be acting as an 'always on' salesperson, ready to talk to anyone who walks through the door...

There are two major kinds of sales pages that you can use in your own marketing to sell your product.

- Long form sales letters

- Video sales letters

Right now, the 'standard' is a video sales letter. There are, every once in a while, applications for long form sales letters but they really are few and far between anymore.

Now, long form sales letter is just that... Long. If you were to print out a sales letter, it'd be anywhere between 12 and 20 pages. We're talking page after page of copy written to persuade someone to buy something...

Now doubt, you've seen them in the past. Some of the world's largest direct response companies have made millions from them.

A few of my favorite examples are:

- The Magic of Making Up
  (http://magicofmakingupcourse.com/presentation_new)

- Stansberry Research - just one of their sales letters is here:
  https://orders.cloudsna.com/chain?cid=MKT042789&eid=MKT277444&snaid=&step=start#AST44101

- Autoresponder Madness
  (https://tinylittlebusinesses.com/email/)

Typically, long form sales letters follow a pretty specific series of elements.

1. **Identify and aggravate the problem.** You first identify that your prospect is having a problem. All of the things we talked about in the Discovery section will come in to play here.

2. **Tell your story.** How are you equipped to help them solve the problem... Is it something you lived through? Do you have experience or education?

3. **Provide a solution.** Share what a solution to their problem looks like and how you solved the problem on your own…

4. **Cover the features and benefits of your solution.** This is where you go into detail on what specific benefits your product or offer will have on your customer's lives…

5. **Your call to action.** The call to action is your "Buy now," or "Add to cart" button. This is also where you'll cover your pricing.

6. **Make a guarantee.** Whether you offer a 30-day money back or 60-day money back guarantee, you'll want to remove any objection that your product will work for your customer.

7. **Scarcity...** The last section should push a specific psychological hot-button prompting them to take action. Examples are, "We only have 500 copies," or "We only have so much time left."

That's the general process for putting together a long form sales letter.

The most important aspects of long form sales letter is the headline, sub-headlines, and buy button. You want them to be attention grabbing and noticeable.

If you're offering a guarantee, you'll also want to make sure you have an image, like a certificate or seal communicating that it's a "30-Day Money Back Guarantee."

You should also include product images, eBook covers, and a picture of yourself and/or your signature at the bottom of the page. That will help lend a bit of credibility and trust through the page.

The Video Sales Letter though... That's a little different. The elements of the page are the same, but they are delivered more formulaically, through video..

Some examples of incredible Video Sales Letters are:

- Lean Belly Breakthrough
  (http://www.leanbellybreakthrough.com/index.html)

- The Lost Ways
  (http://www.thelostways.com/vsl/index.php)

- The Manifestation Miracle
  (https://www.manifestationmiracle.net/)

On these pages, you'll notice that the video plays as soon as you hit the page and there is no video scroll bar, so you can't just skip forward. All you can do is pause the video for a break, and sometimes that functionality is removed too.

The video goes through a PowerPoint presentation, slide after slide, narrated by the 'sales person.' Sometimes it's the product creator. Sometimes it's a voiceover actor.

Video Sales Letters work exceptionally well, converting 1 to 3% of the traffic who hits that page into a customer – much higher than a long form sales letter.

There are two ways to create a Video Sales Letter for your product… You can open up PowerPoint and go to town, or you can walk through the guided sales copy tool inside Scriptly's VSL Creator (http://scriptly.org/vsl-creator/)

If you decide to do it the hard way and write your sales video on your own, here are some notes:

- Writing successful sales copy means you need to:
  o Identify and aggravate the problem
  o Tell your story
  o Provide a solution
  o Tell the prospect how they can get access.
- Include the features and the benefits

- Make sure the call to action is apparent ("buy here" or "click the button.")

- Offer a guarantee (30-day money back, etc.)

- Exit with a "fear-based close."

Once you go through those elements, you'll have the making of a good sales presentation that you can record and publish on your website.

Now, when it comes to publishing your sales video, you'll want to make sure that the pages of your site support it.

The sales video should be front and center, preferably above the fold so it's one of the first things a user sees when they show up to your website.

Here's an example of one of our best performing sales pages:

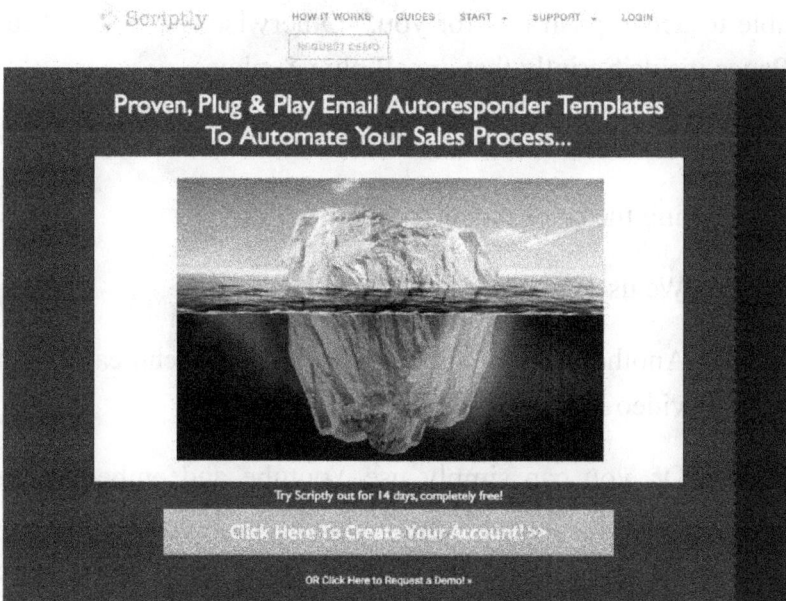

And another…

Now, if you've got a web developer or webmaster, they should be able to accomplish this for you. Otherwise, we've got Video Sales Pages inside Scriptly that are all plug & play.

You can learn more at http://scriptly.org/builder/

For hosting the sales video…

- We use Wistia.com usually.

- Another option, although a bit more technical, is putting the video in an Amazon S3 bucket.

- Or, you can simply use Youtube and embed the video on your site since it's public facing… It doesn't matter who has access to it. It's not like you're trying to limit the number of people who can watch it!

Also, you absolutely must make sure that there is a payment link so your customers can purchase. And, if you're offering a guarantee, make sure that it's written out on the sales page.

Next, we'll talk about creating the confirmation page (or the thank you page) which will be the next step in the sales process for your customers.

That's where you actually give access to the product they purchased.

Confirmation Page

The "confirmation page" or thank you page is where you establish a couple of things... None of them too difficult.

This page is where you:

- Give access to the product that the buyer purchased.

- Thank the customer for their purchase.

- Sign up for product updates

That product update list is going to be a list of buyers, so make sure to give them extra special attention. They're worth a LOT of money to you!

Your buyers list is much more valuable to you than a list of prospects that may or may not be interested in your products in the future. In terms of metrics, a buyers list is usually worth around seven times more more to you than a prospects list.

The thank you page should also inform the customer what is going to be on their bill.

For instance, if you're running ClickBank as your payment processor, then you should include something like "You'll see ClickBank on your credit card bill, not necessarily any clear and cut reference to this product."

ClickBank runs all of the payment processing right through their own merchant, so there isn't a 1-800 number or anything on the bill that relates the buyer to you.

If you are using your own merchant account, like with Authorize.net or Stripe.com, then you'll want to make sure to tell a buyer what will show up on their credit card statement.

NOTE: You will want whatever shows on their statement to reflect your product, not a random name of your business…

Now, there are several different ways to thank your customer for buying your product.

- You can include a thank you video, easily recordable from your webcam or Camtasia. You can walk them through the product, where to download it and the different sections, etc.

- You can just have text on the page saying thank you, and include some different tips on navigating and using the product.

- You can create modules or sections of your course so your new buyers have a way to navigate, starting with the first module...

If you have a video product or a membership site, then your confirmation page is going to do most of the heavy lifting there…

The confirmation page will include a "Register Now" form for customers to create their username and password for your site.

In the next section, we'll discuss the WordPress membership plugin, Wishlist Member. does a lot of the heavy lifting when it comes to creating membership sites. When a customer signs up for access though, it:

- Creates a new user in your membership, granting them access to your content

- Automatically creates their record in your email marketing platform for future updates

- Sends them a confirmation email with access to the course

With your course locked behind a membership registration page, your content is secure and protected… Plus, you can update the product whenever you see fit!

At the end of the day, you should always make it apparent what your customers are paying or have paid for. Give them all the information they need so they won't be surprised when they get their credit card bill. You want them to have your:

- Company name

- Support email address

- Phone number

- Support desk link (if you have one)

Membership

Setting up a membership site if one of my favorite things to do with digital products. It discourages content sharing, and your product ends up neatly tucked behind a membership login screen.

It can be a little harder to set up though.

The easiest way, by far, is to use the WordPress plug-in called WishList Member.

Once WordPress is installed and you're happy with the theme and settings, you'll need to upload and activate the WishList Member plugin. There are a lot of training tutorials on WishList if you need them for reference. It's a paid plugin at $97 for the plugin for one-time access or $297 for developer, multi-site access. It'll save you thousands of dollars in custom programming though.

After you add content (pages and posts – your course material), you then add protect the your material by assigning permissions. Every time a new users is added to the membership site, they're added to the "Level" that they purchased and your content is unlocked.

In order for your members to login, they'll have to go to a special page and put in their username and password that they assigned in the previous step, on the confirmation page.

How I like to set up membership sites is all of the course content is underneath /members/. So, to get access to the material, folks have to navigate to YourDomainName.com/members.

Then root directory (YourDomainName.com) is everything that's available to the public like sales videos, landing pages, blog content, your about page, etc.

If you're like me, you'll have LOTS of promotional material on your website so keeping it separate will reduce clutter and increases security. Every time you go into the member's area, it will all be training content...

Now, in setting up a membership site, there are few things that you need to consider...

1. When will members get access?

2. What will they get access to?

Generally, I try to keep customers engaged with the material which means we'll need to keep fresh content flowing. This is especially important if you want to be able to charge monthly for content. You also want to keep people engaged and coming back to your site. Once they go through the training you've made available, chances are good they'll leave unless you have new content that's being added.

So, adding new content can either be manual... Or automated!

If you choose, you can upload new content every so often. Every week you can throw up a five or ten-minute video. You can do audio recordings, PDF downloads, and some access to other materials.

... Or, you can set up what's called a "Content Drip" or a "Sequential Upgrade" as they call it in Wishlist Member.

Dripping content out week after week, or month after month, you kill two birds with one stone. The membership site unlocks content as if it's new and your members remain engaged! You don't need to do anything manually!

Normally, dripped content is set up weekly. It can also be set up monthly. ... So week by week you members get access to different content. You can do more comprehensive courses or additional training. You can also upsell your members into coaching or consulting.

Another way of keeping your members engaged is by offering a forum or access to a Facebook Group.

Forums are simple enough to set up with another WordPress Plugin, SimplePress Forums. You can provide video training, webinar replays, group coaching, or anything else you might get interest out of to keep people engaged.

Most people would rather do all of their socializing and networking within a portal they're already using... So a Facebook Group is probably your best bet.

Some of the biggest benefits with a membership site are:

- You get to limit access and it eliminates content pirates.

- It gives you the ability to charge monthly, so once people stop payment, their access to the membership-only content is removed, essentially creating a pain of disconnect.

- You get to completely control the environment that you teach including the pages, the pace at which material is unlocked, and the way content is fed to your members.

- Collecting email addresses is easier because it's normally their username.

- You can survey members and ask questions about the content you've provided and the content they want to see next.

- Most importantly, you end up fostering a community and making people feel part of something, which helps them come back over and over.

Building the List

Now, as you go about creating sales material and marketing your course, you'll have a lot of traffic that's hitting your website... Not all of them will buy, unfortunately.

One of the best ways to encourage future sales is to get your prospects to sign up for your email list.

Now, we've already talked about landing pages and squeeze pages in an earlier chapter, but I wanted to spend a minute on why it's important to build an email list and what you should be doing with it...

There are two main ways to build a list:

- Organically through your site's content, referrals, social mentions and search engine traffic.

- With paid traffic (pay per click ads, affiliates, banner ads, etc.)

Typically, the absolute best way to build an email list is to offer something for free – something of value – that your prospects get when the opt-in for your list.

That thing is called your Lead Magnet.

Most often, you set up a landing page offer you freebie, your lead magnet, in exchange for someone's email address. Once they sign up, they get whatever it is you offered them.

Your lead magnet can be one of any number of things:

- Free report

- Video or series of videos

- Free access to a membership site

- A promotional webinar

- Software access

- Printables, spreadsheets, flowcharts

- Process maps

We've used them all in the past. The one that's most common is either the free report or the free video.

We get into a lot more depth on lead magnets, email marketing and email management in the second book in this series, Convert.

For now though, know that your lead magnet has to be high quality and has to be specific to you. The key is to give a prospect a taste of what you do without giving them the overall solution... The solution is the thing we're selling!

It needs to have value though. If it's not worth being sold, folks won't sign up for it just because it's free. Remember, they're giving you their email address which is basically permission to contact them in the future!

The trick is, you want to use your freebie as a precursor to your actual offer, so think of it as a mini product or product preview. It doesn't have to be long... Typically 4 to 6 pages of text or a 5 minute video is all you need. And if you really hate writing, you can edit PLR material from PLRStore.com to create your own freebie report.

... Or you can put together a five or ten article list from Ezinearticles.com or curated content from the Internet that's properly sourced.

You can even put together a small segment of audio answering your most commonly asked questions that are product related... All you have to do is compile your questions, create an audio file, have it transcribed, and release it as a free report.

For email marketing itself, putting your leads on a list and sending email to that list, you can use our service, Convertly. If you go to http://convertly.org/ you can sign up for a free trial.

Infusionsoft, Drip, Aweber and Ontraport are all email marketing services ranging in price and complexity.

Like with the sales page, your Lead Magnet landing page will have a confirmation thanking your prospect from signing up. That's usually the place where they download the lead magnet OR take the next step toward doing business with you. If you decide that the confirmation page needs to be a sales video, deliver the lead magnet through email.

Either way, it's up to you!

Once they're on your list, you can now contact them. What do you do then? I usually follow a schedule like this, all set up in the autoresponder:

1. On day 0, the day they sign up, send them an email with the link to the freebie. Say something like "Hey, thanks for signing up on my list, here is your free report!"

2. On day 1, you want to contact them again and ask them what they thought, and have them fill out a survey. A survey will let them know that their opinions are valuable and they will be able to ask you questions about material they want to know more about.

3. Day 2, after they complete the survey, should be about getting back to them and answering their questions. You can email them and say "Thanks for your input! I am going to do a quick video for you based on the feedback you've provided."

4. Day 3 after they sign up, send an email with a link to the video answering questions you may have received in the survey, and that kind of completes the loop.

5. Day 4, send them to a sales letter link.

6. Day 5, resend the email with a reminder, something like "Have you seen this? Make sure you didn't miss this email!

7. Day 6, send them a few testimonials and talk up the product a bit. Use something like "Some of yesterday's buyers have already had successes, don't you want that success too?"

8. Day 7, another sales letter link.

… Then skip the next three days. Give them a break from the emails until Day 10.

On Day 10, send them a downsell link with a story.

For example, "I have been looking around at the local economic market and there has been so many layoffs in the area. I want you to be a local hero, so here's a link that's going to help you become one!"

Days 11 and 12, send more downsell links.

That a typical scenario for your first 12 days of auto responder copy.

(For Done For You Email Autoresponder copy, make sure you visit http://scriptly.org/video/. Members get the exact sequences we use to make it happen!

Remember, that these people will be on your email list for YEARS if you keep up on it! Maybe they don't buy today or tomorrow or even next week. But they might buy something TWO years down the road!

Typically, what I do then is promote affiliate offers in 3-day sequences. That is just my own personal style.

I'll promote an affiliate offer for three days straight, give them three days off, and repeat. You can easily configure all that right in the auto responder.

It's worked really well for me, so feel free to try the same thing.

You'll also want to make sure to send out a "bonding sequence" where they get to learn a little more about what you do and why you do it. It's a way to "bond" with the reader so your emails are the ones they read...

The trick to successful email marketing is that one sequence should move right into the next.

Remember to always test out different offers in the email sequence as you go, and see what works best for you. Some offers work great. Others don't. You'll want to see what your list responds to and send them more of the same!

Content Marketing

Content marketing has turned into a BIG thing in the last few years. Traffic keeps getting more and more expensive and readers want to feel like they know the person they're buying from… So, a blog can be one of the most effective ways to market and sell your product online.

You should think of your blog as a "content distribution tool" where you teach, talk to and get to know your readers. Now, the way you set up your blog is up to you.

Some business owners post daily. Others post a few times a week. Still others post monthly but make sure their blog posts are extremely high quality. That choice is up to you… But just having one is going to increase the awareness you create for your product or service.

You can treat your blog like your own personal hub; you can write, talk about life experiences, upload pictures, share thoughts, whatever you want.

You can write 200 word posts or 2000 word posts. The sweet spot seems to be 800 to 1000 words. That gives Google plenty of content to index and rank in the search engines, plenty of keyword phrases to rank your content for, and gives your readers something to dig into.

I also recommend that you have a Facebook page setup, where your blog posts get added to the page automatically. There are quite a few WordPress plugins that do that for you automatically; posting to Facebook, Twitter and Linkedin whenever something new is added.

Also on Facebook, one of the BEST things you can do to build your brand and your presence is to do Live Streams or post videos. Live Streams give you a lot of flexibility in the data you collect, so you can put together incredible custom audiences made up of the people who watch a certain chunk of video, creating an audience entirely using Facebook's data!

Another way that people use content to help them sell their stuff is with podcasting. Now, from a functional standpoint, your podcast is set up through your blog. When you attach an .mp3 file to a blog post, iTunes and Google Play see it and consider it a podcast. To pull it off, we use the BluBrry Podcasting Plugin.

Recording the podcast is another matter. We talked earlier about creating audio products... This is a lot like that. You record your voice, a guest, and interview... Whatever. And publish it as an .mp3 file through the BluBrry WordPress Plugin.

In posting that file, iTunes and all the other podcast distribution platforms index the content and automatically send it to everyone who's subscribed. The podcast services, like iTunes, handle all of the syndication for you!

Twitter is also useful in terms of content marketing, but we don't use it that much. It's not that it's falling out of favor, but it's never been a priority for us. If we're going to use Twitter for a client, we're going to run paid ads on it.

Youtube is another place that you can post your content as well. Since Google owns Facebook, it's a great way to easily get ranked for search terms that you couldn't otherwise get. Set up your Facebook Channel. Post videos. Write good descriptions and make sure to post a link to your website or sales page!

Content marketing is where everything comes together. It's a 'hub' of stuff that all supports your product. Whatever you share on your blog should be accessible to your Facebook and Twitter followers, your YouTube subscribers, and anywhere else that you're marketing your product. All these sites feed off the information you put into your blog, so keep it updated with your product information.

Here are some tips on keeping your blog current and impactful:

- Post new material at least twice a week

- Provide valuable content that is going to get clicks, likes, and shares.

- Write content that is useful and thorough for your target market, almost to a point where you feel you're giving away too much. When people read it, they'll know that what you're offering is awesome BECAUSE they're getting so much out of your free stuff.

- Any type of content is good. Text. Audio. Video.

- Show off your personality, expertise, experience and overall knowledge.

- It's smart to do a weekly or bi-weekly audio session and post it as a podcast on iTunes

- In the sidebar of your blog, make sure to add a Facebook like box and an email optin box.

- Make your content sharable, so others can see and learn about you and your products.

Writing Sales Copy

Your products sales copy is the absolute most important thing on your website, because it's actually what is going to make you money. This chapter is going to start the conversation on copy, but it is by no means a detailed expose on converting users.

The second book in this series, Convert, deals exclusively with sales copy and website conversion.

Now, the idea behind your sales copy is that your website is live 24 hours a day. You want to be able to sell a product any time, day or night. Having well-written and always on sales copy makes sure that happens.

Sales copy poses an interesting challenge though...

You need to actually sell something to somebody through text or video.

You're not selling face to face, so there isn't body language or facial expression to feed off of. If you sell something face to face, you can read your prospects body language and facial expression to see what they might be thinking. Online, you can't do that… Which means your copy has to be emotionally and logic based AND you must speak to your prospects aspirations and fears.

Remember when we did the exercises picturing your buyer back in the previous chapters of this book? Where we define your customer avatar?

We talked about:

- How old your prospect was.

- Are they male or female?

- What kind of job do they have?

- What they did when they woke up.

- What they had for breakfast.

- What kind of car they drove.

- How big their family was.

- How much money they made.

This, my friend, is where you use all of that information.

You have to know and understand your prospect's wants, fears and desires.

So when you think about what they want, you need to go deeper than what they tell their wife they want, or what they *should* want. You have to ask yourself, what is it, at the core of their being, do they want?

Do they want to be free? Financially stable? To drive a Lamborghini? Find out.

When you think about their fears, what are they afraid of?

Are they afraid of being broke or disappointing someone? Do they fear failure? Or divorce? Or what other people think about that?

Think about their desires - what they want more than anything else.

When you know the answers, then you're going to be able to write the right sales copy that'll push them over the edge and buy your product.

You need to know why they'd buy, what problems they're facing, what objections they have, and what questions need to be answered.

You need to speak conversationally with them, and put yourself in their situation. Imagine what their reactions will be when they read or watch your sales material.

You should understand that they will be looking for reasons to say no. After all, they most likely didn't wake up this morning thinking that they would be buying your 'thing.'

They will try to find mistakes to reassure themselves. They'll pick apart what you're saying and what they're reading or listening to. They won't want to believe it's actually them you're talking about, but you need to make them feel as if it is. You have to think about the reason they are on your website to begin with, and tap into that.

You can easily tell them that they have permission to say no to you... To not buy... Make it clear that they have a choice. Bring it to their level and say "Look, I think you'll be interested in this. You might not be, and if you aren't, that's fine. But, if you give me a minute, I can tell you how to live a life free of panic attacks. If you're interested, keep reading. If it's not for you, that's okay too."

Traditional direct response copy emphasizes conversion rates and squeezing every last cent out of the buyer. That's not necessarily a good thing, in my opinion. I don't like the fact that video sales letters and direct response marketers are so psychologically keyed in and use advanced tools and strategies like "neurolinguistic programming" or NLP for short.

Some copywriters will say anything to get the sale. They look at conversion rates and say "I need to have a 4% conversion rate or else it's a failure." That's never true. You want to help people solve problems in their lives. Conversion rate is one thing but so is honesty and integrity…

Gary Vaynerchuk spoke at an event I attended recently and he said, "I leave 20% on the table every day, but they buy eventually." He leaves sales on the table, but people come back every day and watch his show and end up buying something from him months or even years later.

That is why we build email lists and market to those folks for the long haul, to make sure our tribe knows we'll be around when they're ready for us!

Two Types Of Sales Letters

Logistically, there are two types of sales letters.

There are Video Sales Letters (VSLs) and there are long copy sales letters (which we have talked about previously).

Video Sales Letters are PowerPoint presentations that are read aloud, slide by slide, and recorded.

Long Form Sales Letters are very long, made up of text and images. Oftentimes, Long Form Sales Letters are anywhere between 10 and 20 pages typed. You don't see as many of them around anymore because sales videos have become the standard and actually convert prospects into buyers more effectively.

… They still work, and they can also be used in a way that video sales letters cannot, which is sent through the mail.

The best way to write a sales video is to sign up for Scriptly's VSL Creator tool at:

http://scriptly.org/vsl-creator/

It'll walk you through the sales copy process step by step and even put the slides and sales copy together for you so you can recorded and get your sales material live and online!

PART FIVE: TRAFFIC

Getting Traffic

The last section of this book is entirely about marketing and getting traffic. It's the "X Factor" in a lot of businesses. You can have a great offer and great sales material, but without traffic you'll never sell anything.

Again, this section isn't an exhaustive exploration of all of the proven ways of getting traffic. There are HUNDREDS of ways to get traffic, some free and some paid.

What I want to do is get you started down a few pathways so you can get some product sold.

The third book in the series, Connect, is entirely about the psychology and implementation of scaling offers, getting traffic, building awareness and connecting with your customers.

So, right now you've created your offer... Your product. It's time to get it launched and out to the public so you can start getting sales.

You've written your sales copy. Your website is up. You just need people to start paying you for your solutions so you can get rolling. In short, you need prospects and buyers. You need people to start getting funneled into your landing pages and sales pages.

After I built my first site, 12 years ago, I blogged day after day for a year... I thought I was doing a good job and I installed Google Analytics to see how much traffic my site was getting. Back then, Analytics was a great tool (and still is) but we built one that I think is a lot easier – http://statly.org.

Anyway, when I first started keeping traffic of how much traffic my site was getting, I was getting about 20 visitors a day. And immediately, I started wondering why weren't more people buying?

At the time, what I didn't understand is that there is something called a "Conversion rate" for sales material. Not EVERYONE buys. In fact, the majority of people DON'T buy.

3% conversion is considered good these days. 4% is great! So for every 100 people that visit your site, you'll get 3 people purchasing your product.

If your sales copy isn't as good as it needs to be, your conversion rate will be closer to 1%, sometimes lower.

That's one of the reasons we like using webinars as sales tools... They conversion much better, sometimes into the 20% and 30% range!

The reason I bring this up now is because a good friend of mine says, "You never have a traffic problem. You have a conversion problem." If your sales copy is converting, you're making plenty of money to pay for traffic. But if it's not converting, you aren't.

It's a Catch 22 though, because you need traffic to test your conversion!

So… right now the biggest thing is just getting traffic. Without traffic, you'll never get a good read on your sales copy and you won't get any buyers… Traffic is where we start.

Now, in the next few sections, we are going to go through a few different marketing methods that are responsible for multi-million dollar campaigns for both well-seasoned business and startups alike.

We'll talk about both free and paid traffic. We'll cover email marketing, solo ads, search engine optimization (organic traffic), getting affiliates, Facebook ads, and Google Adwords. My hope is that one resonates with you and you'll be able to get out there and started on some of it.

… Some traffic can be worked on once, like with a blog post, and you can keep profiting for a long time. Other forms of traffic stop once you run out of ad budget, but are instant to get…

Your List

When we launch something new or when we're working with clients, the first place we market is to the leads we already have… You don't have to pay for them. It's high quality traffic. And you already have a relationship with them.

Not to mention, it's an instant traffic source.

Email marketing is huge for digital business owners in general, whether your promoting coaching offers, digital products… You name it.

You have your list. Affiliates have lists. Bloggers have lists. Some of these email lists can be 50,000 people, 100,000 people, and even 500,000 people! All at the click of a button.

Email marketing is actually a two-pronged traffic source.

- If you're pushing solo ads or affiliate traffic, you'll be getting traffic from other people's email lists

- You'll be emailing your list promoting your offers.

We'll cover affiliates and solo ads in the next section, and concentrate on promoting to your email list here.

When it comes to email marketing and email list management, the first thing you want to do is make sure you're splitting up your buyers and your prospects. They each go on a separate list or are tagged so they're searchable.

Your buyers list will be composed of the people who have already made a purchase with you. You'll want to send them email updates about new content, updates or training calls. Anytime you add something to the course, you'll want to make sure to update your buyers through email.

Then, after two to three weeks of emailing your customers, you may want to start promoting your other offers or affiliate offers.

For example, if you have a product on building greenhouses, you might send an email with a link to a product on creating a hydroponic garden, or an affiliate link to a disaster survival product on the types of food to grow in case of a fallout.

The product might be software, it might be a different viewpoint, or it might be covering the same topic, emphasizing a different section.

Here the thing - buyers who have already purchased your products have already shown you that they buy stuff online. They're comfortable paying for your stuff. And since you know what they bought (or at least your CRM software or shopping cart does) you can use that information to continue sending them other products and services they'll like.

They're probably looking for more information, even after their purchase from you! It doesn't mean your product isn't helpful, just that they're interested in the stuff you teach and want more. After all, pick something you enjoy reading. How many books and magazines are on your bookshelf covering different aspects of that category?

It's rare to have a passion for something and stick to only one source of information about it, so these buyers are going to be on the lookout for more products and services to consume.

THAT'S why your buyers list is worth more to you than your prospect list.

A word of warning though… Try not to crush your buyers with offers. Just because they purchased from you doesn't mean they will continue to if you don't add value to their life in some way.

Promote free stuff to them, like webinars, podcasts, audio sessions, free PDF's, and stuff like that that is monetized in some way on the back end. It ends up being a value for them with the potential to bring you more revenue.

Plus, all of the free stuff that you give away to your buyers builds goodwill and ensures that they continue to open your emails. Your buyers are going to open around 30-40% of the emails you send if you're treating them well. Your prospect list will only open between 15-20%.

Your prospect list is an entirely different story than your buyers list. Some people are ruthless about sending emails to their prospect list, and others are better about not overwhelming them.

By definition, your prospect list is a list of people who haven't purchased anything from you, so some business owners wrongly perceive them as freeloaders. If that's your mindset, it can be a sticky situation.

You have two choices with your prospect list:

- You can either blast them with offers because they haven't spent a dime with you yet

- Or you can nurture your relationship with them, hoping they buy in the future.

The way I treat my prospect list is that they want what we have, what we do, but just haven't been comfortable enough to spend money on anything yet. Or, they haven't seen anything that they've wanted or needed bad enough.

I can't tell you how many people have been on my list for years and years, without doing anything, only to key into our stuff again and buy everything!

This is one of those situations where persistence wins out.

It goes without saying that your buyer list and your prospect list should be treated differently.

Both, however, should be used when you're launching something new because it's the quickest, easiest source of instant traffic you have at your disposal!

Existing Website And Blog Traffic

The next place to go for traffic that you may already have is your blog. Many digital business and digital product owners start with a blog and once they build up their tribe, figure out what to sell them.

To a certain degree, that's how I started selling products. I had a lot of traffic coming to one of my websites for creating slogans, so I created a course for it and posted it online.

To get some insight on what traffic you're getting, you'll want to install an analytics program like Statly, at http://statly.org/.

Statly will give you a comprehensive view of where your traffic is coming from, what pages your readers are visiting, and what they're doing on your site. You're also able to drill down on the individual pages and how they're influencing product sales.

Now, it's likely that only a few pages or a few blog posts are pulling in 80% of the traffic that you're getting. It's truly the 80/20 principle at work. Here are some things you can do to make your products, your offers, a focal point of your content:

- **Add a 'native ad' to your content**, which is like a banner or a callout set in the middle of the blog post. That way, when people are reading, they're invited to engage with you more deeply on the next page.

- **Add a call to action at the end of your blog post** directing readers to your sales page or opt-in page material. If someone finishes the post, they're truly your perfect customer.

- **Put an exit-pop optin box up for people exiting your site.** Good tools to use for this are Picreel.com and Optimonk.com. When people opt-in to your list, put them in a promotional sequence for your product.

- **Add an optin box to the sidebar.** You won't get an incredible number of signups, not like a dedicated squeeze page, but it'll capture folks who are looking for more information about what you do.

- **Post banner ads on your site.** The best use of digital real estate on your website is to promote your stuff, no someone else's! Get some banners made up (or make them yourself) and direct your traffic to your offers.

- **Retarget everyone.** In paid traffic, there's something called a retargeting pixel that you can use to get back in front of your website visitors through paid ads, whether that be web-based banners or Facebook ads. It's always better to have too much data than not enough so retarget every website visitor even if you don't plan on using paid media just yet...

Solo Ads

Solo ads are a great way to get early traffic, especially through the testing phase.

With solo ads, you pay somebody to email their list for you. Your pricing will be driven by how many clicks you get on the email that was sent. Usually you can get solo ad clicks for 30 to 50 cents per click, but that's not set in stone. Buyer lists are more expensive.

Rather than getting an affiliate to mail for you where you pay them a commission per sale, there is no guarantee that you're going to be profitable, because you're paying for the mailing itself.

If you're mailing to 5,000 people you might end up spending $500. But, if you sell 20 or 30 copies of your product, you'll double or triple your ad spend.

Early on, solo ads are how I built my business. It's how I built my list. The first 3,000 or so subscribers I had were all driven by solo ads.

To be sure, solo ads can be a gamble, but it's a pretty straightforward traffic source.

1. You pay for the solo ad.

2. You send the vendor your email copy.

3. They mail the list.

4. You get clicks!

When started buying solo ads, I had a digital product and used the proceeds of that product to buy more solo ads. I would spend $200 for a solo ad and then sell $500 worth of product.

So, I'd take that $500 and buy two solo ads and make $1,000!

You can keep reinvesting the proceeds from the solo ads and build your prospect and buyer list at the same time.

There is also something called a "solo ad swap." Swaps are where you reciprocate mailings for the other person. So essentially, you're emailing their ad to your list, and they're emailing your ad to their list.

I personally don't like ad swaps much because I feel it dilutes my list with people who probably aren't interested in my niche. I'd rather just pay for the spots.

If I can spend $200 and get somebody to mail to their list of 50,000 people and get 1,000 clicks, I end up making great money without worrying about my people be on their list.

For that reason, I tend to avoid ad swaps for the most part. They are an idea if you're just getting started, don't have any money for ad budget, and only have a small 200-300 person list. In that case, you can swap emails with other people and slowly build your list. Once you start making some money with your digital product you should definitely pay for the solo ads themselves.

If you're looking to get solo ads, you can check out:

- **warriorforum.com** - They have a JV section where people post for solo ads.

- **lists.nexmark.com** - There, you'll find a mailing list finder, as it's mostly a search engine. You can search for your niche, and it will show you what lists you can 'rent.'

- **alltop.com** - If the resources we already talked about are a little on the expensive side for right now, you can definitely find something at AllTop, which is the list of the top blogs. You can search for your niche and reach out to website owners direction.

- google.com - Another thing you can do is a Google search for a niche + "powered by Aweber.com." That'll return sites that collect emails.

   On the bottom of every Aweber opt-in box there's a statement that says "Powered by Aweber.com," which is why those sites show up in your search.

With solo ads, it's a good idea to have what's known as "email swipe copy."

An email swipe is a short summary that reflects the actual content that people use in their email to send out to their list. You just send that to the person or company you're buying a solo ad from. It usually includes a couple of paragraphs about the eBook or report you're offering your subscribers. Then you add the link and have it sent out.

You'll also want to make sure to use a tracking link when your solo ad vendors are sending traffic to their email lists so you know how many clicks you're getting.

Public services like Bitly.com will take your long link and compress it into a short link. You can then log into Bitly and track how many times that link is clicked, so you know how many clicks that solo ad sent you.

… Or you can also use a plug-in like 'redirection' for WordPress, which is nicer in my opinion. Just do a Google search to find it.

Lastly for this chapter, a few notes.

- When using Nextmark lists, buy test mailings. Mail to the list's most recently active buyers, and try to mail only to the buyer list. Buy a test of 5,000 people. They email your copy using their servers, so there is nothing you have to set up. If it tests well, continue buying segments of the same list until the response drops.

- Track everything. Make sure to know what good and poor response looks like for your list.

- Keep a list of good solo ad vendors and use them every few months. With email lists, people are always subscribing and unsubscribing so the good vendors will get you more leads!

Search Engines

When people have a problem, they look for an answer. And it just so happens that every answer they could ever want is in their pocket on their smartphone.

With the technology available to us everyday, people are more likely to pull out their phone, ask the connected speaker that's in the room, or open up their laptop *rather* than ask the person next to them.

So, this section is all about getting traffic from search engines like Google, Bing, Yahoo, and the others.

When people search for solutions, answers, to their problems; it means you can be there to help them solve some challenge in their life… To get traffic to your website and to your product if you rank in Google for the keyword in question.

Now, many people think that the results that show up on Google are the best out there, so they're already 'pre-framed' to buy because Google said you had the top result. That's very good news!

Now, combine that with a blog post or a website that helps them answer their question (and others that they hadn't even thought to ask yet), and it's a surefire win for you.

There are a few things you need to actually do in order to get started ranking in search engines though. The first thing is to figure out what people are typing into the search engines.

Step 1: Do Keyword Research

We want to create content and get ranked in the search engine for the specific phrases that people are typing into Google. That content needs to include a link to your product. All the while, making sure that content ranks as high as possible in the search results so people see it.

In short:

1. You find out what people are searching

2. Create content based on those phrases

3. Include links or banner ads to your product

4. Get it ranked in search results, or SERPs for short.

Now, there isn't anything better than free traffic. People rely on Google to find everything… The nearest craft store. How to deep fry a turkey. What's the best price on a stroller they're interested in.

Earlier in the book, we said that typical sales copy gets a 2-3% conversion normally. But when that traffic is coming from a search engine, it's closer to 5-6% conversion because people are in the heat of the moment, looking for an answer right away.

The best thing about search engine traffic though is it's not 'on' or 'off' like paid media. Once you get ranked for a keyword phrase, you'll be getting traffic for a while. There will be competitors that come into the mix, but you can monitor that as long as you don't change much of your ranked content.

Now, there are going to be certain keyword phrases that will be impossible to rank for organically, and that's okay. You can 'buy' rankings through Google, Yahoo, or Bing's paid ads a per click basis, called "pay per click." We'll get into that a little more later.

Search rankings used to be more of a science than anything. You could write content, get a few hundred inbound links, and you'd be ranked. Now though, it's quite a bit more challenging. Still though, you can follow a pretty simple set of guidelines to get it done...

Step 2: Do your market research.

You can use Google's keyword tool and look at what people are searching Google for. The more people looking for something, the better... Within reason of course! The more general of a phrase you pick, the harder it will be to rank for because the competitors on the space will be HUGE companies that have been online for 20+ years. The more specific, the easier to rank but the less traffic you'll get.

If you search Google for "Keyword Planner Tool," you'll be able to create an Adwords account and use Google's on tools. There are others too, such as WordTracker and Spyfu.

With Google's keyword tool, you aren't going to be able to see how many other people are trying to rank for keyword phrases. You also cannot see how many other competing websites there are. For this, you can use a tool called Market Samurai.

Market Samurai is a more specialized tool that can give you a bit more information about the competitors in the market. You can find it at http://marketsamurai.com.

Market Samurai will generate a list of HUNDREDS of keywords that are possible variations of our core keyword, whatever that may be. If you're selling a digital product on getting back together with your ex, your core keyword would be, "how to get your ex back."

If you're selling software to landlords, your core keyword might be, "Property Management Software."

From there, you'll drill down on:

- Adwords cost per click

- Competing websites

- SEO value

- Better variations of the keyword phrase

- Local competition

- Title and Meta tag competition

- And much more!

Once you do the analysis, you'll have a lot more information to use to get some traffic. You'll have a longer list of keywords that you can target with your content. You'll also have a better idea of the competitive landscape in your market.

After you do your keyword scan and do some research, you'll have keyword phrases that you can write an article or a blog post on, publish it to your website, and get it ranked on Google. That's what we're talking about next!

Step 3: Create content for the keyword phrases you've chosen.

To create content that ranks well in Google, you want to follow some guidelines.

- Your article should be between 700 and 1200 words.

- The article needs to have the keyword in the title

- It needs to have the keyword in the first and last paragraph, and the keyword or variations of the keyword need to be sprinkled in the content six to eight times.

- Also, make sure to include at least one image in your blog post.

Then, you post that article to your site or blog!

If you don't have content and you don't have time to write, there's an outsourcing portal that I use at Upwork.com. Articlez.com is another available resource. The best way to get it done is give your writer the specs of the article and the keywords you want inside the writing and then check their work once it's complete.

Step 4: Getting ranked in the search engines.

To get ranked, there are a few things you need to do... You need to build the social aspects of that content and get high quality backlinks.

Before we get there though, there are two things we need to talk about first – On-site SEO and Off-site SEO. On-site SEO has to do with the content that is actually on your site. Off-site SEO is everything that happens outside of your site that is relevant. That includes any outside site linking to yours.

When a website links to your content, Google takes it as a 'vote' for the content that you've shared. Google sees you as an authority; therefore, they rank you higher in the search engine.

The following are ways to artificially get incoming links...

- Social bookmarks are publicly viewable bookmarks that people use to remember websites, such as Delicious.com.

- Social voting lets you express your opinion on a piece of content where you can vote it up or down. A good example is Reddit.com.

- Article marketing can build your link quickly. Article marketing is taking one article (or a spun article) and sending it to hundreds or thousands of sites, getting links back to your content in each article. The most popular article marketing directories are EZineArticles and ArticleDashboard.

In the past few years, Google has went from primarily being fed SEO scores through an algorithm based on On-site SEO and Off-site SEO, where ranking was easy... To a platform that is largely determined by social media votes and shares.

In other words, Google is using real human interaction with a piece of content to predict how good it is and serve it up as search results.

The next time you Google something, click the top organic result. Then, see if there's a social media 'share' or 'like' icon on that article or blog post. I'm betting that there will be and it'll be quite high!

Social media is all about community and the natural byproduct of being part of a community is sharing content. Every time you get a share, retweet, or like of your content, it will show up as a search engine indicator.

Step 5: Rank tracking

The last step of our SEO efforts is rank tracking or "SERP tracking."

So far we have done the research, created the content, built the links, and now we need to track our results. Tracking both your search ranking and traffic will be helpful to clue you in on what you need to do next to rank higher.

For this, you can use a tool like Authority Labs. Google Webmaster Tool is also pretty good if you're just getting started…

Getting Affiliates

Leveraging affiliates is one of the best ways of starting up if you don't have much ad budget or internal traffic to start with. Not to mention, business owners love affiliates because the only time affiliates get paid is when they make a sale!

This can be good and bad, though. The good thing is that you're assured you're making money before they make money... If you give an affiliate 50% commission, then you only ever pay out that 50% when something has sold.

The drawback of paying out an affiliate commission is that often times it's cheaper to pay for traffic straight up. You might only be paying for 15% of your product cost if you're actually buying traffic yourself.

So, if you use affiliates, you'll want to use them at first and then start to implement other traffic strategies that you control and are more cost effective.

A lot of people use affiliate marketing as their sole way of doing business which can be dangerous. When you're counting on someone else to send you sales, you don't really have a good foundation under your belt. What happens when those affiliates no longer have a list? Or they go out of business? Or they decide to stop promoting affiliate offers?

…There is definitely good and bad in having affiliates.

With affiliates, you generally have to pay 50% or above to entice affiliates to promote for you, but you don't pay any other advertising expense. It becomes the affiliate's job to figure out how to advertise your product, and you only pay for what you sell.

Affiliates can drive large amounts of sales, but they also treat what they do as a business… If they send clicks and those clicks don't convert, they'll promote something else. If they send clicks to you and they make lots of money, they'll keep promoting!

Affiliates need to be managed, and that can be a pain. In particular, affiliates are drawn to what they do because it can be a "freedom lifestyle." They make lots of money without working, so they're oftentimes pretty lazy. Getting them to pay proper attention and mail your product can be a process. Once up and running, a lot of product creators hire affiliate managers to do that job for them.

At the end of the day, affiliates are better for short term product tests rather than long term business strategies. In order for you to have a real distribution channel and a real business that will make you money all the time, you'll need to settle on a stable source of traffic portion that isn't rooted just affiliates. In fact, the way I treat revenue generated by affiliates is that it's a bonus… It's nothing to base a long term business model on.

There are in-depth courses on how to get affiliates to promote your product, but it's pretty simple really…

- Promote their stuff first. Most affiliates have their own offers. Land on their leaderboards and get them sales, and then that will spur conversation that will lead to your stuff being promoted.

- Go to events and meet people in the industry. Don't engage in conversation about your products yet. You don't want to turn them off by giving them the vibe that you just want to use them. If you just introduce yourself, hang out, and make yourself a part of the conversation, it will lead to connecting with those people after the event, creating working relationships and talking about products through email or social media.

- Promote the fact that you're good at something. Whether it's writing a sales copy, knowledge in a certain subject area, or whatever else, helping someone out speaks volumes about your character and sets up trust. Do a favor for someone without expectation and they may offer to mail for you.

- Have a page on your site that introduces affiliates to your product(s) and lets them sign up to promote.

One good strategy is to let affiliates include some of your content as a bonus with theirs…

Let's say you create an ebook or a video course that's about woodworking. Any forum, digital product, website or membership that's about working with wood could give away your content to all it's buyers/members, growing your customer base.

… No one will turn down free content or the chance to put quality information on their site that they didn't have to write themselves!

Let's say this woodworking website owner sold 20,000 copies of their product, 5,000 of those people seeing your free stuff. All of those folks already showed that they're interested in paying for information, and some of it was from you! A certain percentage of them will cross the line over to you and buy what you're offering!

The bottom line with getting affiliates is you have to be willing to give before you receive. You don't want to ask them if they'll promote you right away, before you've done anything for them. It's about building the relationship between yourself and the affiliates that you would like promoting your offers.

Creating free content and sending them sales is only going to benefit you in the long run. You simply have to continue cultivating that relationship.

One of the biggest things you can do though is make it easy for them to promote you. You want your affiliates to mail for you in a timely manner, put banners on their sites, and send you sales and traffic. The more you do for your affiliate, the more likely they are to mail for you without hesitation.

Create email templates that they can just copy and paste into their auto responder and mail out. Include links their affiliate links for them. Customize the email copy a little for their niche. Make sure they understand your promo sequence, what's expected of them, and when they'll get paid.

Keeping affiliates on track is a huge responsibility. You'll want to add your affiliates to a separate email list and include an opt-in box on your affiliate page for them to get 'affiliate only email updates.'

Once you find yourself dealing with affiliates a couple of hours a day and it begins to monopolize your time, that's when you should begin to look for an affiliate manager. A good affiliate manager actually has relationships with affiliates, and manages your affiliates for you. They can also expose your products to other affiliates that they have relationships with.

Having a good affiliate manager often pays for itself in no time because their job is to get you sales and you're no longer spending time on that particular part of your business.

Generally, affiliate managers work for a percentage of total commissions and the better ones require a retainer. For example, they might ask for $2,500 per month retainer with 10% earnings of the sales that they bring in. That's also only 10% off the top, not 10% of your share. That, of course, is something you'll discuss with the affiliate manager before you get started with them!

Facebook Ads

The idea behind Facebook marketing is to serve targeted advertisements to Facebook's user base. The brilliant part about it is that Facebook has more data on each and every one of its members than any other advertising platform in existence.

You can target anything and everything you want, including:

- Relationship status
- Location
- Preferences
- Life events
- Likes
- Dislikes
- Favorite books
- Favorite movies
- Music
- Celebrities
- Liked pages
- And more!

You can target any of these people based on what they're interested in, and then advertise to them.

Earlier, when we did our keyword research on "how to get your ex back," we saw how many people searched for those terms. With Facebook ads, we can target people based on a recent change in their relationship status; single men, single women, divorced men and women, and anyone else who fits the bill.

With Facebook ads, you'll have an image and some ad copy. It's set up like a normal status update but will include the little, "Sponsored" tag on it in your prospect's newsfeed.

- The image should to be related to the product, something that's preferably on the landing page of the ad.

- The copy of the ad itself shouldn't be pushy, but should be rather conversational. People aren't necessarily looking to be sold to while on Facebook.

- The ad needs to be more attention grabbing than promotional. Remember, people log into Facebook to chat with friends and see what people are doing, not be advertised to.

- You'll be paying per click or per thousand impressions, but you want to avoid making the actual sales ad pushy or direct response oriented.

On the landing page your Facebook traffic is directed to, you should clearly state what you're going to do with the email address. Facebook has really been cracking down on this, making it required to post your Privacy Policy and Terms of Service on the page.

You shouldn't expect a Facebook user to click an ad, go to a site, and directly purchase a $97 per month program. It's interruption-based advertising.

You should have a buffer, which is where your promotional material comes in.

Use free content; establish your credibility and then work on selling them your digital product through email or retargeted ads after they opt-in to your marketing.

There are lots of different types of ads in Facebook but they boil down to two main types. Facebook ads are billed either on a cost per click basis or a cost per thousand impressions (CPM).

Every time somebody clicks on an ad with cost per click, you'll get charged. With cost per impression, you'll get charged when the ad is triggered 1,000 times.

For beginners, it's worthwhile to start with a 'cost per click campaign,' and then move it to a 'CPM campaign.'

You can get started with Facebook ads at http://facebook.com/ads/. If you don't already have an account, you'll need to create one.

Based on the information we went through before about branding yourself, you should already have an account and a Facebook page set up. From there, setting up a Facebook ad is pretty straightforward.

Google Adwords

Google Adwords has been the standard in paid advertising for a long time, but their recent rule changes have led to a lot of people leaving their ranks.

Google has two basic types of as platforms, contextual and search.

Contextual ads show on Google's publisher network sites, which is basically anywhere that is showing AdSense ads. That might be blogs, forums, download sites or free tools that are monetizing their traffic with Google's Adsense platform.

Those sites have the ability to serve any of Google's ads on their site. For instance, if a blog post is about penny stocks and you have a penny stock product, your ad can show up on their website. It allows you to buy traffic from a lot of different sites without having to go and contact each of the sites individually. It's much cheaper to run contextual ads, but the click through is often a bit lower.

The search network is served through Google's properties. Ads show up on search pages on Google's search network. You can see these ads anytime you go to Google and type in a search term.

Let's say you go to Google and type in "How to get your ex back." You'll end up seeing ads at the top and bottom of the search results, all of which are paid ads. You can see them clear as day because they say "Sponsored" somewhere around the listing.

When you see that, a business has gone into the Adwords platform and paid to advertise their product in Google's search pages when someone searches for any number of keyword phrases.

Many business owners will pay to have people click on their ads and land on their page. But, if they aren't selling anything, why bring them to the landing page or the site in the first place?

To get approved in Adwords, you'll have to make sure your site is complete and that the ad will have the potential to turn a visitor into into a buyer.

(For more on that, read the next book in the series, Convert.)

Google has really cut down on the number of paid ads they're showing because:

- They want to give their users the best experience possible, and...

- There were people driving Adwords traffic towards some misleading content and websites.

So, Google put a stop to it, banning a lot of advertisers from using their platform. The result is a platform that is more restrictive BUT serves better quality ads. In fact, they have a "Quality Score" associated with every ad on their network. The higher the score, the less you pay per click.

Now, Google allows for both text based and banner advertising.

Text based ads showcase a headline, description and a click through URL. Your text-based ads will show us in both search and contextual and all center around the quality score given to the ad, analyzing your ad text, your landing page, and a bunch of different metrics that calculate price per click and ad relevance.

In order to do a good test, you'll need to try a few different ads out in order to see what works, and you'll need a budget of $500 to $1,000 in order to really dial in the campaigns.

Banner ads are big block-like images that show up in their contextual network of publisher sites. Banner ads are a little bit more lenient in terms of approval. The quality of the landing page is still calculated through the quality score, but you get more access to traffic through banners. The downside to working with banners as your ad medium, testing a lot of different variations can get expensive unless you're creating them yourself.

The perfect storm in Adwords is running banners in the contextual network. The banner will need to conjure emotion, and should be related to the #1 issue your customer avatar is facing before they purchase your product. You always want to sell the next action - not the product itself.

Pretty looking banners don't necessarily outsell ugly banners, so keep that in mind when testing stuff out through Google.

PART SIX: AUTOMATING THE FUNNEL

Building Your Sales Funnel

The most successful business online don't just have one product, they have product lines. Those product lines are sold continuously around the clock through a sales funnel.

After your first product is successfully launched, you'll want to figure out what you're going to do next.

Really go deep in your niche and figure out what problems you can solve in your market... A market you already have a presence in. Maybe, it's expanding into other consumption formats like Kindle Books, iBooks, speaking gigs, coaching or consulting. You really want to branch into other areas without having to reinvent the wheel with new products all the time.

We've already talked about the offers you can create in this book... All you need to do is go back through the pages and figure out what you want to sell next!

By now you have tested your product, you're driving traffic to it, and making money. You can begin to expand your reach to include to more buyers and different groups of prospects, which might involve getting a little uncomfortable and branching out of your current space.

Most of the time, after a product owner proves that their product works, they go out and create something else right away....

Now, I'm not saying that having multiple products in the pipeline isn't good, but why not wring as much money as you can out of the market you're currently in with the product and product line you currently have?

The key to making a fortune selling your stuff is to find as many people as you can, in a way that's evergreen and automated. You sell the same product with new people constantly getting added into your sales funnel.

That, my friend is the beauty of a web based business.

You create something once. You sell it again and again.

To do that though, the pages of your website need to be written and structured in a certain way... When someone hits your website, they need to know what they should be doing next.

That might be:

- Downloading a free report

- Signing up for and attending a webinar

- Watching a sales video

- Signing up for a strategy session or a sales call.

You want your website working for you 24 hours a day, 7 days a week.

Engineering that sales process is where the second book in this series, *Convert*, comes into play.

You'll discover how to convert your prospects into sales following a proven, automated sales funnel formula geared for conversion. By following the models in this book, you'll learn how to sell pretty much anything, in any vertical or niche, regardless of price.

You'll find out:

- How to sell to your prospects using webinars and virtual, automated events…

- The right price for your offer online (cheaper isn't always better!)

- The right way to structure your email marketing sequences to maximize conversion while still focusing on automation…

- How to choose the right software for the job… Solutions that are easy to set up and robust enough to work in the most stringent of scenarios.

- How to create complicated upsells paths so you're always selling the 'next' thing to your customers…

- How to get your website visitors to give you their email address, letting you reach out to them in the future with email marketing!

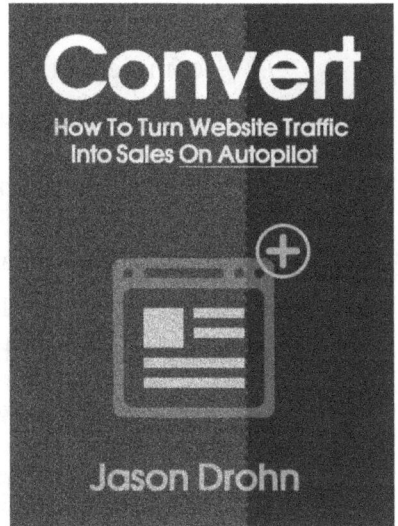

- How to sell high-ticket coaching, consulting or highly complex offers online, without ever needing to meet your prospect face to face!

- Plus so much more...

Convert is a book that you will highlight and use as your digital marketing roadmap for years to come, no matter what your experience level is at the moment...

Pick up a copy here:

http://jasondrohn.com/convert/

Conclusion

There you have it, some of my best stuff on creating offers to sell online.

Of course, I can't possibly put everything there is to know about Internet marketing and offer creation in one book, so I have focused on the main ways you can start and grow your web-based business profitably.

You may stumble upon a way that works for you, like mobile apps, click arbitrage or joint ventures that isn't covered here... Or you might put something together that's a combination of a few offer types.

My hope is that you've enjoyed reading this book and learned from it, but more importantly, I hope you take action and implement what it teaches. After all, just reading about offers and startups won't do anything for your business until you act on what you've learned.

To schedule a call for a customized action plan for your business, go to:

http://doneforyou.com/schedule/

And finally, come check out our software, Scriptly.org, Curately.org, and TimeSlots.org; see the About the Author page for more details.

Jason Drohn is an Erie, PA-based entrepreneur and the creator of several software solutions to save you time and make your business more efficient, including:

Scriptly.org

Generates email sequences and other marketing materials and builds your landing pages for many purposes.

Statly.org

Analytics and sales funnel tracking platform to give you more insight into the traffic that's hitting your site and the sales channels that are driving revenue.

Askly.org

Survey and quiz platform created to help business owners get better insight into what their prospects and customers want from them, for development and marketing.

Convertly.org

Email marketing software for businesses and website owners, delivering email marketing and automation that just works…

Curately.org

Curates content for your website in minutes.

TimeSlots.org

Easy scheduling, especially for coaching and other high-ticket services.

He is also the founder of **DoneForYou.com**, which creates a variety of custom marketing solutions for companies in many different niches and industries. If you would like to work with him and his team, visit DoneForYou.com.

www.ingramcontent.com/pod-product-compliance
Lightning Source LLC
Chambersburg PA
CBHW061156240326
R18026500001B/R180265PG41519CBX00009B/11